Conversations with Feminism

Conversations with Feminism

Political Theory and Practice

PENNY A. WEISS

ROWMAN & LITTLEFIELD PUBLISHERS, INC.
Lanham • Boulder • New York • Oxford

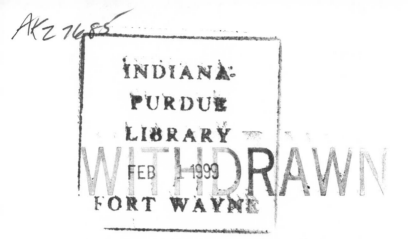
ROWMAN & LITTLEFIELD PUBLISHERS, INC.

Published in the United States of America
by Rowman & Littlefield Publishers, Inc.
4720 Boston Way, Lanham, Maryland 20706

12 Hid's Copse Road
Cummor Hill, Oxford OX2 9JJ, England

British Library Cataloguing in Publication Information Available

Library of Congress Cataloging-in-Publication Data

Weiss, Penny A.
  Conversations with feminism : political theory and practice / Penny A.
Weiss.
    p.   cm.
  Includes bibliographical references.
  ISBN 0-8476-8811-9 (cloth : alk. paper).—ISBN 0-8476-8812-7 (pbk. : alk.
paper)
    1. Feminist theory.   2. Feminism.   I. Title.
HQ1190.W464   1998
305.42'01—dc21   97-30124

ISBN 0-8476-8811-9 (cloth : alk. paper)
ISBN 0-8476-8812-7 (pbk. : alk. paper)

Printed in the United States of America

∞ ™ The paper used in this publication meets the minimum requirements of
American National Standard for Information Sciences—Permanence of Paper
for Printed Library Materials, ANSI Z39.48—1984.

*To the next generation of conversationalists,
especially my children and my students.
Talk isn't always cheap.*

Contents

Preface

My desire to construct conversations no doubt has some of its origins in the fact that I am from a family in which various members frequently stopped talking to one another and in which I was sometimes the one everybody did speak to. I have come to see my ability to communicate across conflict and confusion, and to encourage others to do the same, as a form of strength, an ability I can put to good use. This project is one of my attempts to put it to such use.

That there are conflicts between feminists and antifeminists is clear enough. The two groups are assumed to have different beliefs, positions, and policy preferences on virtually all issues having to do with gender, from the Equal Rights Amendment and abortion rights to women in the military and parental leave programs. They are expected to differ in others ways, also, since some associate the divide between feminists and antifeminists with other divides that go beyond gender: liberals vs. conservatives, for example, or Democrats vs. Republicans, or religious "fundamentalists" vs. religious "reformers."

Conflicts within feminism are, perhaps, more visible to those in the movement than to those outside it. In fact, those outside feminism tend to portray it as a monolithic whole, ruled by a sort of creed to which all its "members" must pledge allegiance. But there most surely are internal disputes. Those disputes may be voiced in different theoretical frameworks (liberal feminism vs. radical feminism, vs. Marxist feminism, vs. socialist feminism, vs. black feminism, vs. lesbian feminism, vs. ecofeminism, etc.). The internal conflicts may be expressed over policies (should we aim to ban pornography, to make its producers accountable for harm it encourages, or to reform and reclaim erotica?), strategies (should we pin our hopes on the Democratic party, start a third women's party, or work outside party politics altogether?), and particular ideas (is "woman's nature" a figment of the male imagination, a product of socialization, or the source of values for an egalitarian future?). Finally, disputes arise about which women feminists are talking with and about: is feminism really "white middle-class feminism," and if so, how do we transform it into something more inclusive and respectful of differences among women?

This book did not begin with the thought that I should write a book of conversations with(in) feminism. But it occurred to me one day in the middle of a class I was teaching that such conversations were what I was always engaged in: in speaking and teaching I saw/see myself practicing, refining, using, and sharing ways to discuss controversial issues involving feminism, and in thinking and writing I realize(d) these dialogues were my way of processing and conveying various subjects. I'm sure these practices are not unique to me.

This book began with my going back over papers I had written (or, more often, started to write) to see how many were in fact conversations of various sorts. Many were; sometimes when I made that more explicit, the whole essay made more sense. And once I saw that, I was able to write more, to use the idea of conversation to discuss other issues I had wanted to write about. This collection is united by a commitment to dialogue as part (not the whole) of feminist ethics, strategy, and pedagogy.

The part of my first book, *Gendered Community: Rousseau, Sex, and Politics*, on which I have received the most feedback is the dedication. (I don't think too much about what that says about the rest of the book.) What people comment on is my honesty about such things as rejected manuscripts and the impossibility of "balancing" career and parenthood. I won't go over that terrain again, though I still get manuscripts rejected and I still beat my head against the wall trying to do (not *have*) it all.

Between these covers is a decade of work. Reflected here are my struggles, especially with teaching and with my chosen field of political theory. I am fundamentally ambivalent about my job. I have tried a hundred different ways to make it work for me. I have tried lectures and student-led classes, the big conferences with thousands of political scientists of all stripes, and the small, specialized meetings. I have tried being involved in university politics and withdrawing from them, immersing myself in my work and just doing my job. As with strategies for child rearing, because something works once does not mean it will work again. I think that my long engagement in political dialogue has tired me, which is something I probably should but do not develop much in this book.

I dedicate this book to those I have had the pleasure and difficulty of conversing with in recent years. I especially want to acknowledge my friends at The New Community School in Lafayette, Indiana, with whom I have learned so much about education. Most of all, to those I talk at, with, to, and about every day: Avian, Brennin, Linden, and Bob. I am still learning to converse, and I mean to keep practicing with you. Here's to a future of good conversations.

1

\# \# \#

Conversation as Method

conversation, n. 1. knowledge or familiarity based on study
or use. 2. a talking together; informal or familiar talk; verbal
exchange of ideas, information, etc.
Syn.—talk, intercourse, communion, communication, discourse, conference, colloquy.

C onversation first emerged in this project as a practice rather
than a theory of political investigation. But what seemed to
begin as a personal writing style evolved into my method
of exploring and expressing political ideas. Conversation—beyond
the model of Socratic dialogue—might deserve some status as a
method in political theory. Here I present some thoughts on what
defines conversation as a method of inquiry and how it contrasts
with some other practices.

From my first impressions of political theory, I have understood
conversation broadly, encompassing a range of forms of interaction. (Aristotle wrestled with the popular opinions of his day. The
characters in Plato's dialogues most obviously were talking to each
other. Aquinas translated Aristotle for a new, Christian audience.
And so on.) Some conversations in this book are set up between
different theories or theorists, including an exchange between feminism and communitarianism and a scripted dialogue between

Rousseau and Wollstonecraft. In one piece the silence of women in theoretical discourse is itself the subject. Another is a response to letters in the form of a letter to Abigail Adams. Other conversations are my attempts to communicate with antifeminists and nonfeminists. Some have me talking to myself. As I introduce each piece, I say something about the conversations contained within it.

What idea of conversation brings these essays together? First, like most of the real conversations we have in life, the tone is generally informal, or at least more informal than is the norm for political theorists. (I once had a manuscript rejected because, the editor said, I "write too much like people talk.") But I believe that true conversation invites people to join in, and the more inaccessible the language and the more foreign the tone, the more that invitation is meaningless, and it might as well have gone unsent.

Second, all the essays arise from and are framed by a genuine desire to have different voices confront each other, exchange ideas, listen, and speak. The goal of this method is always to establish something interactive, dynamic, alive, two-way. A conversational approach informed by feminism does not, contrary to some stereotypes, preclude disagreement or contrasting stories; in fact, as Marilyn Frye argues, it requires them.[1]

Third, one of the aspects of conversation I value most is that in conversation the process by which we arrive at our positions is more visible than it is when we only present formal arguments in support of our already arrived-at conclusions (a standard form of academic writing). The invisibility of the process contributes to the widespread impression that political theory is almost incomprehensible for most people, for the starting points are unmarked, as are too many of the lines that connect later dots. At times, making the process visible can make an essay seem slow-moving or obvious. But if these effects are deemed to be defects, rather than virtues, of the method, those defects, I believe, are outweighed by other positive consequences.

Much of political theory is done via methods I would consider antithetical to conversation. The adversary method creates contest, winners and losers, not conversation, and it leaves out all those intimidated by it or who find it a questionable means to better knowledge.[2] Refutation aims only to show what is wrong with a treatise, not what in it may also be right and useful, making one-up"man"ship, rather than cooperative exchange, too much the object. Overly abstract or technical approaches exclude identifiable groups from the discourse, making the works partial, and systematically so (as can works that constantly presume that the reader has read everything that the writer has read). Most works called political theory more resemble lecture classes with one teacher and a room full of passive learners than interactive seminars filled with people in multiple roles as teachers and learners. Minority views are invited in only when the majority finds them useful.

To converse one has to be conversant with the topics. The pieces in this collection, for all the attempt at accessibility, do assume some familiarity with political theory. Too, the norms of the university dictate that I use endnotes—preferably lots of them—and that the references be mostly to other academic material. I know that can be a problem, can make a reader feel as if they do not understand the point if they do not make sense of the notes, too. But some of the essays here have no notes, and no meanings are hidden in notes that do appear.

To converse also means simply to talk freely together. Simply? True conversation demands both listening and speaking skills. It requires open-mindedness, patience, a degree of safety, and a willingness to change. To listen to others means sometimes to quiet oneself. To speak to others means sometimes to feel unsure, vulnerable. Audre Lorde wrote, "I have come to believe over and over again that what is most important to me must be spoken, made verbal and shared, even at the risk of having it bruised or misunderstood."[3] Feminist writings throughout history seem to anticipate being misunderstood. For example, the authors of the 1848 Declaration of Sentiments, adopted at a women's rights convention in Seneca Falls, New York, concluded their document by saying, "In entering upon the great work before us, we anticipate no small amount of misconception, misrepresentation, and ridicule; but we shall use every instrumentality within our power to effect our object."

Some misunderstanding happens because of the distance between one person's mouth and another person's ears. Some of it happens because of the complexity of the subject or the lack of clarity with which it is presented. The scariest sort happens from a will to disbelieve, to disprove, in situations in which the reader/listener has something at stake in the writer/speaker's being wrong.

Perhaps what is most opposed to conversation—to conversing—is silencing. *Silence* as a noun can mean calmness and peace. But *silence* as a verb can also mean to make silent; to cause to be silent; to oppose or refute with arguments that are unanswerable; to put out of action; to restrain in reference to liberty of speech. The silencing I am concerned with is a political phenomenon that can manifest itself in an endless number of forms, as Susan Griffin explains:

> Our silence. The silence and the silencing of women. The creation of authority in the image of the male. Of god in the image of the male. Rape. The burning of witches. Wife-beating. Laws against women speaking in public places. Against women preaching. The imprisonment of suffragists. Force-feeding. Harassment on the public street. Scorn for the woman who dares to *act like a man*. A woman's love for another woman, unspoken, hidden. Our invisibility in history. The manuscripts of Sappho burned, the writing of women never published, lives of genius spent obscurely, or in domestic labor and childrearing; the life of the mother, of the housekeeper, unimagined and unrecognized. Woman's word pronounced full of guile. A woman's testimony held suspect in court.[4]

Such silencing is aimed at identifiable people and viewpoints. If those who are supposed to be silenced continue to speak, they may be punished. Political silencing calls certain voices illegitimate, unimportant, dangerous, and uninformed. It allows other voices to become deafening.

Writing of lesbianism, Charlotte Bunch says:

> One tendency in this country is indeed to deal with "problem populations" by trying to get them out of sight. A territory, a ghetto, a closet, a jail or mental hospital—anywhere, so long as it is not necessary to look at and treat "them" as human beings.[5]

By extension, if such people must be seen, they will not be heard.

The ability of some to engage in conversation has, with frightening regularity in history, been seen by others as a threat. Marlene Nourbese Philip reminds us of this.[6]

> EDICT I
> Every owner of slaves shall, wherever possible, ensure that his slaves belong to as many ethno-linguistic groups as possible. If they cannot speak to each other, they cannot then foment rebellion and revolution. (56)
> EDICT II
> Every slave caught speaking his native language shall be severely punished. Where necessary, removal of the tongue is recommended. (58)
> absencelosstears laughter grief / in any language / the same / only larger / for the silence / monstrosity / obscenity / tongueless wonder / blackened stump of a tongue / torn / out / withered / petrified / burnt / on the pyres of silence. (92)

Philip knows silencing as a weapon used against some to protect the privilege, the illegitimate power, of others, and the machine that perpetuates such privilege. It knows no limits. She portrays the silenced as unable to talk, even with each other; punished for speaking, sometimes hideously so; and absent.

It is easiest not to hear the silenced, especially if the verbal space they might have occupied is taken up by noisy others. Those who do the silencing are portrayed by Philip as owners and, despite their control of others, as still feeling threatened and thus capable of brutality. Both the silenced and the silencers are monstrous.

The politics of silencing is a high-stakes game, filled with rules and rituals that make it seem lawful and fair. It creates familiar structures that are not easily or individually overcome. Silencers must give up some forms of control, must risk what we have, must look at some as fully human who, until now, have been something less than our equals. We must learn to be silent ourselves and to listen. The silenced, on the other hand, in some cases need not only to give voice to our thoughts but to formulate thoughts once too dangerous to allow to develop. Our well-founded distrust must be transformed. The silenced must get used to being seen, noticed, heard, responded to. We must learn Lorde's lesson: "My silences had not protected me. Your silence will not protect you."[7] What have the conversational norms really been protecting?

Silence seems to have both aural and visual dimensions. The silenced are not only muted but invisible to those who speak. Their absence goes unnoticed. The conversation continues without them, sometimes with great sincerity and effort (sometimes not), and its incompleteness, its biases, also go unnoticed.

Silencing is profound and pervasive. How can it end when the speakers feel no absence, hear no quiet, when the silenced lose their voices? The silenced cannot be spoken for and must not just be spoken about.

I cannot imagine a soul alive who has never felt what it is to be silenced—even the most powerful were once children, students, apprentices, or newcomers or became old or less able than they were. That common experience can, with hard work, goodwill, and risk, become the basis of common knowledge. The most talkative among us today can recall the costs of being silenced and can recognize the processes that enabled it to happen. From that knowledge must then come action for change.

I also cannot imagine a soul alive who has never articulated, even if to him- or herself, their own thoughts. As James Scott documents, the oppressed commonly talk in "hidden transcripts," expressing often "heretical" ideas and feelings out of the sight or earshot of the oppressor.[8] That history contains another beginning, for in it can be found some confidence, some tradition, and some community. Here, too, is a place from which action can arise.

My goals here are modest and in most cases are approached more by examples than grand or abstract theories. Or, being more generous to myself and my project, the theory of conversation is applied in what follows in a number of different ways, to a range of people and ideas. For example, I use Plato to try to make women's absence visible and something that matters. I use Rousseau and Wollstonecraft to make plain that women are part of classic conversations in political thought, even if many pretend to partial deafness. I use Hill and Thomas to show that even words we struggle for can participate in the exclusion of others. Such methods, if they should be called that (I probably, in the end, prefer "strategies"), demand careful attention to texts, ideas, and authors. They also allow those writings, thoughts, and people to move into new contexts, new conversations with new acquaintances and audiences, giving them and us new ways to gain and shed light.

> *Talking with one another is loving one another.*
> —African proverb

Notes

1. Marilyn Frye, "The Possibility of Feminist Theory," in *Theoretical Perspectives on Sexual Difference*, ed. Deborah Rhode (New Haven, Conn.: Yale University Press, 1990), 174–84.

2. See, for example, Janice Moulton, "A Paradigm of Philosophy: The Adversary Method," in *Discovering Reality: Feminist Perspectives on Epistemology, Metaphysics, Methodology, and Philosophy of Science*, ed. Sandra Harding and Merrill B. Hintikka (Dordrecht, Holland: Reidel, 1983), 149–64.

3. Audre Lorde, "The Transformation of Silence into Language and Action," in Lorde, *Sister Outsider: Essays & Speeches by Audre Lorde* (Freedom, Calif.: Crossing Press, 1984), 40.

4. Susan Griffin, *Pornography and Silence: Culture's Revenge against Nature* (New York: Harper & Row, 1981), 201.

5. Charlotte Bunch, "Speaking Out, Reaching Out," *Passionate Politics* (New York: St. Martin's, 1987), 204.

6. The following quotes are from Marlene Nourbese Philip's intriguing *She Tries Her Tongue, Her Silence Softly Breaks* (Charlottetown, Prince Edward Island: Ragweed Press, 1989).

7. Lorde, "The Transformation of Silence," 41.

8. James Scott, *Domination and the Arts of Resistance* (New Haven, Conn.: Yale University Press, 1990).

"I'm Not a Feminist, But . . ."

I guess that almost everyone with a strong commitment to feminism has wanted to tear their hair out (or someone else's) in response to yet another person uttering a phrase such as "I'm not a feminist, but . . ." In this essay I try to understand and respond to the reasons people give for distancing themselves from feminism even as they identify with various feminist positions.

The conversation in this piece is between feminists and nonfeminists, represented here by me and authors I use, and groups of my students, respectively. I asked my students for their ideas about resistance to feminism. Then they did the talking. I took their written words and oral comments and came up with responses to them. I shared this essay with the students I surveyed. They seemed moved by it, seemed to recognize themselves and to understand my responses to them.

One thing I learned in writing this essay is that the myths about feminism are not simply either true or false. There are layers of meanings in and multiple interpretations of each one. Discovering that opens up the possiblity for dialogue between feminists and nonfeminists. Another interesting thing I learned is that what people shy away from is not feminism but the consequences outside of feminism of being seen as a feminist.

Patriarchy perpetuates its deception through myth. . . . Myths are said to be stories that express intuitive insights and relate the activities of the gods. The mythical figures are symbols. These, it is said, open up depths of reality otherwise closed to "us." It is not usually suggested that they close off depths of reality which would otherwise be open to us.

Mary Daly, *Gyn/Ecology*

2

❦ ❦ ❦

"I'm Not a Feminist, But . . .":
Popular Myths about Feminism

T he *Daily Collegian* polled 364 randomly selected women at
Pennsylvania State University in 1991. It found that a respectable 38.2 percent of the women consider themselves
feminists. But an extraordinary 96.8 percent say they support gender equality on social, political, and economic levels.[1] Some 58.6
percent of the women responding were clearly trying to distance
themselves from feminism, even as they showed support for various feminist positions. The difference between these figures war-
rants explanation.

Disclaimers such as "I'm no women's libber" are very common.
I remember a time when I, too used such a disclaimer, memorable
because I was challenged to reflect on it. As an undergraduate at
the University of South Florida, I had to meet with my political
science professor, who was, somewhat surprisingly for 1974, a
woman. In the course of conversation, and for reasons now unknown to me, she asked whether I was a feminist. There I was, a
first-generation college student, sitting in a small office with "A
Professor." This was neither a familiar nor a particularly comfortable experience for me. What was I supposed to say? I fell back on
the safest, most familiar response I could conjure up on the spur of
the moment: "Well, I'm not a feminist, but I believe in equal pay."

In 1974, as I rattled off to my professor the things I believed in even though I was *not* a feminist, she said, "Oh, well, if you believe in that, then you *are* a feminist!" Hmmm, I thought, give me some time to think that over.

Since that time I have heard many say "I'm not a feminist, but . . ." with various endings to the sentence: "I'm not a feminist, but I believe in equal rights"; "I'm not a feminist, but I wouldn't tell my wife she had to stay home and take care of the kids"; "I'm not a feminist, but I think women and men ought to be whatever they want to be"; "I'm not a feminist, but I don't think violence against women is right." Like my professor, I sometimes say, "Oh, well, if you think that, then you *are* a feminist." And I get back the same skeptical looks I'm quite certain I gave her.

After more than two decades of engagement in feminist politics, teaching, writing, speaking, and living, I find myself concerned to understand that reluctance and discomfort so many feel with saying, "Yes, I'm a feminist." After all, it seems unlikely that any significant percentage of those women surveyed by the *Daily Collegian* would say, "I don't eat meat, but I'm not a vegetarian," or "I'm not a Democrat, but I believe in the Democratic Party platform." What is at stake, then, in rejecting or adopting the label "feminist"?

One semester I asked my undergraduate "Women and the Law" class to help me out. On the first day of class this nonrandom sample[2] of Purdue students broke into small groups and came up with separate lists of the reasons people say, "I'm not a feminist, but . . ." My class divided themselves into fourteen groups of from two to five people. They wrote down what they came up with and turned the lists in anonymously. Grouping their responses, I found the following:

- Nine groups cited the fact that feminists are perceived as radical, which means, according to their notes, too radical, against tradition, too liberal, wanting to change everything, wanting too much.
- Seven groups cited concern with social rejection: society does not condone outspoken women; feminists will be outcasts in a male-dominated society; they will be rejected by men and/or

society; they will offend, will end up arguing, will lose men's respect, will be perceived as pushy bitches, and might lose their jobs.

- Seven groups raised issues around sexuality, noting that feminists are identified as lesbians. One group, using *gay* rather than *lesbian*, perhaps acknowledged the possibility that men might be feminists, too, and those men too would be perceived as homosexual.
- Seven groups associated the reluctance to call ourselves feminists with social norms of masculinity and femininity, five saying feminists are unfeminine or downright masculine, two additional groups noting that feminist men were perceived as feminine or wimps.
- Four mentioned that feminists are seen as antimale, man hating, or wanting to be dominant over men.
- Finally, four cited varied issues of style: feminists are associated, again according to their notes, with being outspoken, aggressive, macho, pushy, one-sided, narrow-minded, hard-line, cold, and harsh.

To what extent are the popular perceptions of feminism, as described by my students, accurate representations of feminist theory and practice? Why do certain myths and misconceptions exist—that is, how do they arise, and what functions do they serve?

The first noteworthy aspect of my students' responses was the degree of overlap in their lists. Without question, popular images of feminism and of feminists surround us. I think no one has managed to avoid them. A different semester I asked students to tell me what a feminist was like, and, to my surprise, they were able to come up with not only ideas about her political views but also stereotypes about everything from the shoes she wore and the haircut she sported to the food she ate, the pets she owned, and the books she read (vegetarian, cats, Alice Walker . . .)! The popular image is not only pervasive but also fairly detailed.

Most important, the popular image is largely a negative one, at least as judged by current social standards. Just how negatively and how costly feminism is seen to be is revealed by the number citing social rejection as part of their reluctance to endorse feminism. When are people most afraid of rejection? Perhaps it is when we care deeply about being accepted or when the consequences of rejection are dire. It is important to be clear here about who finds feminism unacceptable. What was most often mentioned by my students was that power structures, such as those in the world of paid labor, and people with power, namely men, would reject feminist women. Much of what is called fear of feminism is in fact fear of men, of what men might do or not do to women who somehow don't comply. The widespread existence of this fear is indicative of women's more vulnerable social and economic status, their dependence on males and male approval. This fear is all too real. The problem, however, is not the horror or the unacceptability of feminism itself but the horrible power of the status quo to punish what it deems unacceptable so that it may maintain itself. It is not so much that a woman thinks it horrible to challenge a boss who sexually harasses her, or to protest government cuts in Aid to Families with Dependent Children (AFDC), or to leave a husband who abuses her, or to question the ethos of domination that continually brings us to the brink of war. No, it is not feminism itself that is being called unacceptable. What is unacceptable, what is horrible, is that if she challenges her boss for sexual harassment, she will be fired, or be called delusional, or be told she asked for it, or be ostracized by her coworkers; if she protests the poverty of female-headed households, she will be treated as embodying or endorsing laziness and promiscuity; if she leaves her abusive husband, she'll be asked what she did to provoke him, or he will successfully pursue her and the police will say they cannot do anything; and if she challenges the military mentality, she will be called unpatriotic.

Feminism is unaccepted by too many with too much power, making feminists unacceptable and the costs of feminist identification and living real. That message has been heard, loud and clear. Much less visible to too many with both too much and too little power are the costs of antifeminism: rape, domestic violence, self-hatred, poverty, and lost potential, to name but a few. Equally as indistinct are the rewards of feminism. But how incredibly, wonderfully, powerfully real these gain are: relations of friendship between equals, true partnerships with our lovers, the restoration of our confidence in our own power, the reclaiming of our self-worth, the rejection of violence and exclusivity, and the integrity of the constant challenges presented by forsaking destructive sexist patterns. So, yes, there is some truth in the popular understanding that feminism is unacceptable, but a misperception persists that it is the tenets and practices of feminism itself that make it so, rather than those self-protective self-interested behaviors and structures of the status quo that reward conformity and punish resisters. Opportunities to evaluate and explore feminism openly are too few, so quickly and deeply has it been cast in a negative light by many well-respected individuals and institutions. Yet when we allow their judgment to become ours and shun identification with feminism, we leave the myths intact; we accept as valid the cat's version of the troublemaking mouse.

Antifeminism has had a larger part than has feminism in shaping popular perceptions of feminism. Judging by my students' comments, one of the most successful antifeminist themes has been that feminism is radical. The fact that feminism is understood as radical may be an unspoken acknowledgment that antifeminism is, very much, the status quo. If feminism wants to change antifeminism, and if feminism wants, as my students said, to change everything, then antifeminism must be pervasive. This acknowledgment is reminiscent of a court case in which a woman was being tried for the death of her extremely abusive husband. The judge said he was not going to give women licenses to kill their husbands. His fear was that if one woman got away with this, women everywhere would start killing their husbands. At some level he understood that huge numbers of women are being battered in their homes and that the criminal justice system is useless or counterproductive to them, which is why the prospect of battered women defending themselves so alarmed him.[3] The extent to which feminism seems and is radical is relative to the extent to which the norm is antifeminist. Or, as Pat Mainardi puts it in an article on sharing housework, "The measure of your oppression is his resistance."[4]

Calling something radical is often an indirect way of writing something off or challenging its legitimacy. Whether the group being labeled is war protesters, civil rights activists, animal rights advocates, union organizers, or feminists, calling them radical is a way of saying, "I don't have to think about what they're saying, do I? I don't have to change the way *I'm* doing things, do I? After all, they're so radical." This sort of dismissal through name-calling might reveal that the ideas being called radical are hitting something too close to home or something a little scary; something in which we have a vested interest, or something we have already declared decided. We thus desire to brush off this radical challenge as we do any intrusive or dangerous pest.

Etymologically, *radical* means "to the root." Feminist analysis that goes to the deep structural roots of gender identity and oppression inevitably forces us to rethink our ideas, restructure our institutions, review our daily practices, reconceive our relationships, reevaluate our mores, and revise our ideals. Systemic oppression based on sex, race, class, nationality, and sexuality will survive any less radical efforts. That is why we would rather brush feminism off as radical. It both seems like and is a lot of work. Furthermore, in our current framework of values, radical feminism is asking us to work for things we've been taught to understand as relatively unimportant. You know, feminists always make mountains out of molehills. What's the big deal, after all, about rape, when our culture teaches that women enjoy it? Why should we change the way we speak of women as objects when our culture teaches us to see this as flattery? Why should we care about job discrimination when our culture teaches us that women would really rather not be employed for pay anyway? Consequently, before we can convince people to change those things that contribute to the creation of dominant males and subordinant females, we first have to make the subordination of women something problematic. The highest authorities in every field have declared that women like their subordination: it's woman's nature; it's for their own good; it's all that can be expected; it's not really so bad. It is only against such a background and in such a context that feminism looks, and indeed is, radical. How radical feminism is stands as a measure of how patriarchal a society we confront. Feminism seems radical because, looking at the same event, feminists see subordination, injustice, and serious offense, while others will only reluctantly, if at all, see a misdemeanor of little consequence.

From another angle, there is nothing very radical about feminism. It is an expression of the time-honored, self-evident truth that we are all created equal (even if the authors of the Declaration of Independence forgot to use gender-inclusive language, the Constitution forgot to include women and minority men as full citizens, and it wasn't until 1971 that the Supreme Court first struck down a sex-based law as unconstitutional). Feminists want women and men to be treated with equal respect; to be given equal opportunity to express their potential and to be appreciated for their contribution; to have choices about the families they create, the jobs they hold, and the partnerships they form; and to have personal, social, economic, and political resources at work to eliminate exploitation, discrimination, oppression, abuse, and violence. This long and still incomplete list presents a very full conception of equality, a very inclusive and enabling conception. Not so easy to attain, perhaps, but clearly a worthy and admirable goal. Why, then, the ridicule of feminism, the titters about "those bra-burning libbers"?

To understand that we can look again at my students' responses. Seven groups cited issues of sexuality, and, related, seven mentioned norms of masculinity and femininity. I think we titter when we're nervous. And I think the reason we titter about feminism is because we're nervous about crossing those sacred boundaries that separate men from women everywhere but the private bedroom (where there is nervousness about the sexes *being* separated). Norms of masculinity, femininity, and heterosexuality are among the most powerful in our culture. Calling a man effeminate or a woman masculine or mannish is a serious accusation meant to provoke negative, disapproving, wary response. Talk about ex-president George Bush as a wimp, as effeminate, seriously offended him in a way that criticism of his Middle East policy or his lack of commitment to accessible medical care did not, as *Newsweek* magazine found out after its campaign cover story on Bush called "The Wimp Factor." His references to "kicking ass" in response to situations ranging from his vice-presidential debate with Geraldine Ferraro to his showdown with Saddam Hussain are in part attempts to reassert his manhood, his masculinity. Something seriously unfunny was thought to be at stake.

It is true that feminism challenges the sacred boundaries here, violating the clearly and pervasively disseminated social requirement that there be two distinct, sharply polarized, and hierarchically arranged sexes. The male feminist wimp (among others), as my students noted, is someone who fails to fulfill this requirement in his life or in his politics. A wimp is a man who betrays men by refusing to be a bully to women. He's "henpecked," the only alternative to the exertion of masculine privilege our culture can manage to imagine. When they refuse to exert power over women, we call men wimps; we call them what is a dirty name in our society; we nab them for the crime of refusing to be real men. Real men dominate women. To be a man is to dominate women. And to be a real woman is to accept that domination, in at least some arenas on some levels, to live every day in quiet subjugation to men on the streets who harass us for their entertainment, to men on the job who underpay us for their profit, and to men at home who take advantage of us because it's become second nature. Systems of oppression justify this abuse, and those on top try to buy others off with worthless compensations in an attempt to mask and perpetuate the systemic privileges that work against us.

Maintaining the boundaries of masculinity and femininity, and of heterosexuality, are central tasks of education and public policy, of advertising and pornography, of fashion and storybooks. We are witnesses to the channeling of our economic, social, political, and psychic resources into maintaining male privilege. These boundaries define the sexes as different and men as better, making it absolutely essential to cross them and tear them down. In doing so we reject defining all human beings in terms of their sex and all human relationships in terms of power. The power relationship between women and men obligates the members of one sex to harass, abuse, exploit, ignore, or ridicule the members of the other sex, who must acquiesce or at least limit their complaints to forms that are "appropriate" and therefore ultimately ineffective. It is made incumbent upon us to prove our manhood and womanhood repeatedly throughout our lives—every time we dress ourselves, get a flat tire, initiate a conversation, eat, or play games. In these and other situations, men prove their manhood by being taller, smarter, tougher, more competent, richer, cooler, more athletic, or more powerful than women, who prove their womanhood through subservience, nurturing, acquiescence, understanding, accommodation, incompetence, and weakness. To be a proper female, to be feminine, is to be disempowered.

And to be a female, to be feminine, is certainly also to be heterosexual, because to be a lesbian is to reject men and male rule, to question the myth that women need men, and to exist as a dangerous example, a challenge to patriarchy by being a woman yet *not* being subservient to a man, by refusing men access.[5]

When people say of feminists, "Oh, they're just a bunch of dykes," they are engaged in another variety of attempt at dismissal. The speaker of these words intends to write off all the claims of feminists by feeding on people's fears and prejudices about homosexuality. They hope to send shivers of horror up the spines of women who might be feminists, who might challenge the status quo, by warning them of the cost—the stigmatization that will follow. They hope, and often succeed, in scaring women into taking less radical stands and in making all alliances between women and for women's interests inherently suspect. Because the lesbian label is a powerful weapon wielded against feminists, challenging the norm of heterosexuality is a project critical to feminism. Our most popular model of sexuality demands male control over women, thus using sexuality to help keep women in their second-class seats.

When we hesitate to identify as feminists because we fear breaking sex-specific rules about what is masculine and feminine, about what is fitting for women and what is fitting for men, what we are leaving intact are those rules that actually create us as dominant males and subjugated females. And, yes, challenging the division of practically everything in the world—from colors and toys to names and professions—into masculine and feminine is frightening, because we are challenging something very fundamental to our social system: its organization within and on a framework of sexual differentiation and inequality.

My students are right in another sense, this is to say, about the radicalness of feminism. Many feminists argue that sexual inequality affects much more than relations between the sexes: it bolsters, borrows from, provides a model for, and trains folks in other forms of domination, competition, and selfishness. Our ideology justifies or explains away wife abuse and, similarly, the abuse of natural resources. The system that denies the need for mandatory paid parental leave policies is well trained to ignore the needs of the homeless. The system that can make rape women's fault can make affirmative action reverse discrimination. A system of sexual differentiation that forces us to think of women and men as us and them prepares us well to create numerous divisions and hierarchies around the globe.

Most social systems, like most individuals, operate by instinct, training, or habit in such a way as to protect themselves. Present many organisms with something that threatens it, and it fights or flees, tries to stay as it is, to adapt as little as it must to survive. This defensive behavior belongs as much to humans as to bugs, as much to democratic regimes as to despotic ones, as much to systems of sexual equality as to ones of male dominance. Staying power never made anything right, though, or even speaks to unusual strength. That's just how systems generally work. And, unfortunately, there's nothing inevitable about habits having to change or to change for the better. Patriarchy has shown itself to be quite adaptable, able to withstand numerous assaults and challenges throughout its history with relatively minor modifications.

By patriarchy's self-(pre)serving definitions of what is hateful and monstrous, feminists are indeed monsters: macho, pushy, narrow-minded man haters. Our feelings toward men, individually or as a group, positive or negative, have precious little to do with why we are portrayed as antimale. We live in a culture in which to be female and to do other than be subservient to men is said to be man hating. When women do something with their energy and their lives besides serve men, padding male egos and their paychecks, putting up with their remarks and their demands, then women are called man hating. When women stand up for themselves and demand a certain level of treatment, they are called man-hating. When a woman refuses to submit, she is said not to love men. Looking carefully at the actions and the attitudes that are labeled man hating shows that they have very little to do with hating men and a great deal to do with challenging male rule over and access to women. Only when to be loving is defined as to be self-sacrificing, long-suffering, uncomplaining, and acquiescent to men is feminism anti-male. But it is not man hating to have strengths of one's own, ideas of one's own, work of one's own, and love for oneself. It is a lie that the only way to love men, or anyone, is to serve them, as a master, a god, a superior. It is a lie that we *should* love those who demand such tyrannical terms. How far man hating is from what we are about, and how little it captures of feminism, of the injustice of the status quo, of the imagination and passion of its resisters.

Mary Daly writes:

> Even the most cautious and circumspect feminist writings are described [as antimale]. The cliche is not only unimaginative but deadeningly, deafeningly, deceptive—making real hearing of what radical feminists are saying difficult, at times even for ourselves. Women and our kind . . . are the real but unacknowledged objects of attack, victimized as The Enemy of patriarchy—of all its wars, of all its professions. . . . The contemporary facts of brutal gang rape, of wife-beating, of overt and subliminal psychic lobotomizing—all are available. What then can the label *anti-male* possibly mean when applied to works that expose these facts and invite women to free our Selves? The fact is that the labelers do not intend to convey a rational meaning, nor to elicit a thinking process, but rather to block thinking. They do intend the label to carry a deep emotive message, triggering implanted fears . . . freezing our minds. For to write an "anti-male" book is to utter the ultimate blasphemy.[6]

In actions that others call antimale, feminists are demanding a revision of what it means to love oneself and others. Feminists *are* antimale when the only other option is subordinating oneself to men. An analogy may be helpful here. When someone says, "Feminists have no sense of humor," a complete understanding of and response to the accusation includes recognition of the fact that much of what has passed for "jokes" are put-downs of women, sexist and often racist, one of the numerous means by which women are kept in their place. Our refusal to laugh along does not signal an impoverished sense of humor but reflects a refusal to contribute to our oppression by ridiculing ourselves, perpetuating precisely those stereotypes that are then all too effectively turned right back against us. We need to be more critical about the effects of our socially constructed sense of what is funny, just as we need to be more critical of the effects of our socially constructed understanding of love. We *should* reject those relationships that demand or contribute to our subjugation, even if they pretend to do so in the name of love or laughs. This does not mean, by the way, that we are not very loving and very funny.

Myths are often somewhat contradictory: the same feminists who supposedly hate men also supposedly want to be men. Nonetheless, when it is said of feminists that we want to be men, again there is some truth and much falseness in the claim. On this issue, too, it is important to look at when this claim is made. When we want to wear comfortable clothing, it is said that we dress like men, as if men had a monopoly on loose clothing, comfortable shoes, and easy-to-care-for hairdos. But to reject as unhealthy shoes that injure our spines, to reject as contributing to our victimization training that makes us unable to flee, and to reject as contributing to our objectification skirts in which freedom of motion is an impossibility, is not to reject being a woman! It is, instead, a most healthy, self-affirming assertion of our worth as full human beings. When we want certain jobs, we are said to be taking them from men, as if men had a monopoly on the need for money or the desire and ability for certain tasks. The demand that women not engage in these "male" practices is an admission that being a woman in a male-dominant society means being injured, victimized, objectified, and underemployed.

Yet all this does not mean that feminists are working to be what men have been. To challenge certain male monopolies is not to voice acceptance of the way things have been done, structured, distributed, evaluated, or rewarded. Feminists do not think there is anything wrong with being a woman. But it is wrong that if you are a woman in a patriarchal society you should expect to have not only to sit in the back of the bus, so to speak, but to sit there with an attractive smile on, prepared to sweep up after the menfolk depart.

Last, then, to the question of style: the perception of feminists as aggressive, pushy, and macho. These accusations are a call for women to be more patient, not to want so much so soon, and to be nicer when asking for change. Martin Luther King, Jr. was told by so-called moderates that he should be more patient in his demand for racial equality, because change is slow. He responded:

> They will say this even about freedom rides, they will say this about sit-ins; that you're pushing things too fast—cool off—time will work these problems out. Well, evolution may work in the biological realm, and in that area Darwin was right. But when you seek to apply evolution to the whole fabric of society there is no truth in it. Even a superficial look at history shows that social progress never rolls in on the wheels of inevitability. It comes through the tireless effort and the persistent work of dedicated individuals.[7]

Another civil rights worker, this one in the age of U.S. slavery, William Lloyd Garrison, wrote, "[I]s there not cause for severity? I will be as harsh as truth and as uncompromising as justice. On this subject, I do not wish to think, or speak, or write with moderation. No! No! Tell [one] whose house is on fire, to give a moderate alarm?"[8]

Every day that sexism continues, every day that women are oppressed across the globe, women are battered, raped, denied, confined, and killed. They are told who they can love and under what conditions, how many children they must bear and how they must raise them, where they can work and where they can safely walk. As King and Garrison argued, moderation and patience are inappropriate, self-defeating demands issued by those most desirous of the least change. It is, I know, unladylike to be so demanding, skeptical, and insistent. "Pleasing femininity" is self-denial. There is an urgency to feminist demands, and although it is true that change seldom happens overnight, that must not be allowed to become an excuse for inaction and the continuation of injustice. We had best not provide so easy an out for those who would just as soon see oppression continue. Patience and understanding, those great feminine virtues, can also be our enemies.

When I told my professor, "I'm not a feminist, but . . .," I was allowing the myths about feminism to cloud my own understanding of fairness and equality and my own best interest. I was allowing those who gain from sexism to invalidate the truths I knew from my own life. I still marvel today at the phenomenon: that we uncritically accept the untruths told us about the evils of feminism and uncritically reject the truths told us by feminists about patriarchy. It is testimony to the power of culture that we can come to believe that feminists are man haters, that feminists are antifamily, that feminists are mean-spirited and harsh; and also that we can come to believe the lies about life in patriarchy: that women enjoy being raped, that women stay in abusive relationships because they like it, and that women who say no mean yes. Amazingly, it is easier to believe that her no meant yes than that her no meant no. In the absence of a context that is thoroughly patriarchal, anti-woman, a context we can only imagine and strive for, these and similar beliefs would be seen immediately as destructive lies that serve the supposed interests of some at the real expense of others. Sexual inequality educates us in polarization, rationalization, exclusion, competition, and violence.

Today I myself am a college professor, and that's why I'm a feminist. Because I still hear in the stories of my students the pain and loss of sexism, and I see the difference it makes for them to learn about and practice resistance to sexism. Today I am in the fourteenth year of a relationship with my partner, and that's why I'm a feminist. Feminism provides our relationship with more honesty, more challenge, and more richness than does any other single factor. Today I am the mother of three children, and that's why I'm a feminist. Because I see in the future of my son and two daughters the greatest hope for peace, opportunity, and justice in feminism. So today I have no reservations, no "buts." Professor Stoudinger, wherever you are, if you ask me today whether I'm a feminist, my answer is "Yes, you bet, no question about it, of course, isn't everyone?"

Notes

Versions of this chapter have been presented at Ball State University, at the Purdue Women's Studies Symposium at Purdue University, and as a convocation address at Manchester College.

1. The results of this survey are reported in "Shying from the Stereotype: Feminist Movement May Suffer as Today's Students Shun Label," *U.: The National College Newspaper* 4 (March 1991): 1–2. Also see "I'm Not A Feminist, But . . ." in the November 1992 issue.

2. The sample might be thought to be more "liberal" than most given that it is composed of a majority of young, college-educated women. It might also be thought of as more "conservative" than other groups, since most of the class was white, midwestern, and middle-class. The lack of a random sample means what follows should not be seen as an exhaustive list of answers. But that the answers included are common is, I think, unquestionable. Also see Barbara Smith, "Some Home Truths on the Contemporary Black Feminist Movement," *The Black Scholar* (April 1995): 4–13. Smith discusses some of the same myths, some different ones.

3. Sharon Wyse, "She's Battered; Judged Guilty," *New Directions for Women* 17 (July/August 1988), 1.

4. Pat Mainardi, "The Politics of Housework," in *Sisterhood Is Powerful*, ed. Robin Morgan (New York: Vintage Books, 1970), 447–54.

5. See Marilyn Frye, "Some Reflections on Separatism and Power," in *The Politics of Reality: Essays in Feminist Theory* (Trumansburg, N.Y.: Crossing, 1983), 95–109.

6. Mary Daly, *Gyn/Ecology: The Metaethics of Radical Feminism* (Boston: Beacon, 1978), 27–28.

7. Martin Luther King, Jr., commencement address delivered at Lincoln University on June 6, 1961, reprinted in *Great American Political Thinkers*, vol. 2, ed. Bernard E. Brown (New York, Avon, 1983), 413.

8. "Commencement of the Liberator," in *The Writings and Speeches of William Lloyd Garrison* (Boston: Wallcut, 1852), 63, reprinted in *Great American Political Thinkers*, 10–11.

Toward Theories of Antifeminism

More than any other in the collection, this essay is an attempt to set up a framework that would facilitate conversation between feminists and antifeminists. This was actually the first piece I ever wrote after completing my doctoral dissertation on Rousseau. That dissertation was a long attempt to understand and ultimately to refute Rousseau's defense of sexual differentiation. In this piece, I take that same approach to judicial and congressional support of sex roles. What concerns lay behind such support? How might one talk to someone on the other side?

In terms of conversations about this piece, a funny thing happened. Some people said it was about time we focused more attention on antifeminists, that not enough of us were doing it, that that is where the real battle is to be fought. Others said it was a useless gesture, that we should frame and discuss our own issues on our own terms. It reminded me of hearing one person say to me, as a child, that I looked just like my mother, and the next person saying I was the spitting image of my father. In both cases there is truth on both sides.

> But it is pointless to write off the antifeminist woman as brain-washed, or self-hating, or the like. I believe that feminism must imply an imaginative identification with all women (and with the ghostly woman in all men) and that the feminist must, because she can, extend this act of the imagination as far as possible.
>
> Adrienne Rich, "The Antifeminist Woman"

3

🌿 🌿 🌿

Toward Theories of Antifeminism: Judicial and Congressional Defenses of Sexual Differentiation

Over the last decade or so we have witnessed the awesome proliferation of feminist theories. A current list of theoretical frameworks for understanding and ending women's oppression would include at least liberal, radical, socialist and Marxist feminism, cultural, lesbian, black, postmodern and ecofeminism. With this daunting list in tow, it is clear that we spend a lot of time arguing among ourselves over such issues as whether the cause of women's oppression is ultimately rooted in ignorance, sexuality, or economics and whether "woman" is a class, a caste, or a group too diverse to lend itself to any neat generalizations.

These debates, of course, are essential to the building of sound, inclusive feminist theory. However, perhaps we now spend so much time in internal dialogue that we spend insufficient time arguing with the "real enemy," the "other side"—the antifeminists.

Given that we are neither masochists nor "traitors," why should feminist theorists *want* to talk with antifeminists? There are good reasons for thinking it important to have an accurate, fair, and complete picture of antifeminism. First, continuing discourse with the opponents of feminism can add theoretical strength to our posi-

tions, by pointing us to issues we haven't perceived or fully addressed. Second, taking their concerns seriously, we can uncover
common ground where it exists. Where it does not, we can respond
to those concerns more directly, perhaps persuading some along
the way, and thus increasing feminism's political viability. That is,
I am concerned with the costs for feminism of incorrectly understanding antifeminists. In general, if one misperceives one's opponent, one may be unprepared for their attack, may lose
opportunities to negotiate peacefully with them, may unwittingly
or needlessly back them into a corner, or lose opportunities to work
with and educate them.

I think we too often quickly dismiss all antifeminists as unrepen-
tant, unreasoning misogynists whose sole concern is preserving
male privilege and the world modeled on male values at any cost.
I am not denying that some antifeminism is merely reactionary or
solely an attempt to empower some at the expense of others. I am
simply claiming that we cannot assume this is always the case. We
need a more sophisticated understanding of the range of concerns
and assumptions that lie behind and inform the opposition to feminism.

I am interested in antifeminism as an ideology that defends the
sexual division of labor as personally and/or socially beneficial and
as reasonably equal and just. The questions I want to ask include
"What do antifeminists fear?"; "Why do they cling so fervently to
what they call 'traditional values'?"; "Why do they view changes
in the family as dangerous?"; and "What is their understanding of
human nature, of human psychology, of economics and politics?"
As the self-appointed Freud of the opposition, I wonder, "What *do*
antifeminists want?"[1]

In this essay I explore two broad arenas in which antifeminist
reasoning is explicitly laid out by its own adherents. First, I look at
U.S. court cases in which differential treatment of the sexes has been
upheld and cases in which various nontraditional family arrangements have been condemned. There is sufficient material in the history of the law's treatment of women to give rise to anger and
amazement among even those with the most modest of feminist

sensibilities, and, indeed, those laws helped spur feminist political activism.[2]

> Voting rights, jury service, right to a separate domicile, causes of action for loss of consortium, capacity to enter into binding agreements and to sue and be sued, change in citizenship upon marriage to an alien, change of name upon marriage, age of attaining majority— these are only a few of the many areas in which a person's sex has at times made the sole difference in the treatment he or she would receive under the law in the United States and other countries.[3]

Most forms of discrimination against women have found expression in law. As Tocqueville said, "There is hardly a political question in the United States which does not sooner or later turn into a judicial one."[4] As one fine strand of the web that both mirrors and reinforces society's view of proper sex roles and relations, antifeminism in the law can give us information about the views of antifeminism in general.

I also explore congressional and popular opposition to three pieces of proposed legislation that can fairly unproblematically be said to be supported by most feminists: the 1963 Equal Pay Act, the 1971 Child Advocacy Bill, which proposed a national network of preschool child care centers, and the Equal Rights Amendment (ERA). In all three cases, of course, some opposition was based on technical aspects of the bill—enforcement problems or administrative details, for example. But much was not; the bills were more often explicitly linked with perceptions of feminism. And the opposition did not hesitate to engage in all sorts of hyperbole. The measures were called "revolutionary," "deeply radical," "dangerous," and "an invitation to legal and social chaos." They were associated with everything from totalitarianism, socialism, and Hitler's Germany, to Huxley's *Brave New World*, Orwell's *1984*, and Skinners's *Walden II*. What follows is an attempt to grapple with just what was so fearsome about the legislation to its antifeminist opponents.

My focus is on the theories to which antifeminists have appealed and on the values and concerns to which they have given voice. In these court opinions and legislative debates I find three distinct, though overlapping concerns. The first, which has its roots in biological determinism, is a concern with the social efficiency of sex roles; the second, which is grounded in a view of the liberal capitalist marketplace, raises issues about the emotional importance of women's traditional role; and the third, based on an understanding of human moral tendencies, gives voice to concerns about the moral security and stability arising from sex roles. In discussing each of these, my goals are to point out the biological, psychological, social, moral, and/or economic assumptions being made by antifeminists and to conclude each section with thoughts about what questions feminist theory needs to discuss in response.

Biological Determinism

Briefly stated, biological determinism holds that biological, and consequent psychological, emotional, and intellectual differences, fit the sexes for different social roles that society rightly enforces as leading to personal happiness and social order. Biological determinism sees many human capacities as biologically determined and the sexual division of labor as the natural outgrowth of sex differences. Traditional gender roles are understood as either inevitable or preferable, and departures from them are held to cause social inefficiency and personal unhappiness.

Court cases from the nineteenth and twentieth centuries often cite arguments rooted in biological determinism. In 1873 the Supreme Court upheld an Illinois law denying women eligibility to practice law. The Court held that the practice of law in state courts is not a privilege of citizenship protected by the Constitution. Justice Bradley's famous concurring opinion focused on the privileges of "women as citizens to engage in any and every profession." These might be different from those of men, in part because of the "natural and proper *timidity and delicacy* which belongs to the female sex, [which] evidently unfits it for many of the occupations of civil life."[5] In *Muller v. Oregon* in 1908, the Supreme Court upheld an Oregon law limiting women's working hours in mechanical establishments, factories, or laundries to ten hours a day. This "interference with the right and liberty of the individual to contract" her labor was defended (though it was not upheld for men in *Lochner v. New York*) on the basis of "[t]he differences between the sexes." Sex-based legislation was constitutional because "The two sexes differ in *structure of body*, . . . in the amount of *physical strength*, in the capacity for long-continued labor, particularly when done standing, [and] the influence of vigorous health upon the future well-being of the race."[6]

In *Radice v. New York* in 1924 the Court upheld a prohibition against employing women in restaurants in large cities between 10 p.m. and 6 a.m. against a due process challenge based on the liberty of contract. The law was held to be a proper exercise of state police power because "night work is substantially and especially detrimental to the health of women . . . considering their *more delicate organism*."[7] In 1977 the Court upheld a policy restricting women from being correctional counselors in maximum-security institutions for contact positions. A woman's ability to do her job, it was decided, "could be directly reduced by her womanhood. There is a basis in fact for expecting that sex offenders who have criminally *assaulted women* in the past would be moved to do so again."[8] And in the 1981 case of *Michael M. v. Sonoma County*, the Court upheld a statutory rape law in which only females can be victims and only males can be violators because "only women may *become pregnant* and they suffer disproportionately the profound *physical, emotional, and psychological* consequences of sexual activity."[9]

Each of these cases asserts that the sexes are simply different and that laws granting different jobs, working conditions, and liabilities to the sexes on the basis of these differences are reasonable and just. In the Aristotelean words of the Court, the law does not require "things which are different in fact . . . to be treated in law as though they were the same" (*Michael M. v. Somona County*). These cases seem to show that whether sex-based laws are challenged under Title VII, the due process clause, or the equal protection clause, whether they concern civil or criminal matters, and whether they are heard in 1873 or 1981, an appeal to sex differences can be used to uphold them.

Opposition to the legislation noted here also appeals in part to biological determinism. Regarding the proposal for government-sponsored child care centers, an article included in the *Congressional Record* noted, "In the first place, mothers should be home with children from 0 to 6 years of age. They need their mothers for the zillion things that only mothers can do. . . . [N]obody can ever replace a child's mother."[10] Another asks, " 'What's wrong with mothers staying home and raising their children in their own homes?' More jobs would then be available for fathers. Our nation became the most progressive, productive and free nation on earth when this procedure was followed."[11] Opponents of the Equal Pay Act talked of the "extra costs" business already bears in hiring female employees, which "arise from the indisputable fact that women are more prone to homemaking and motherhood than men."[12] (In fact, even some proponents of the bill stressed that while there were positions "which men and women can perform with equal ability, [in which] there should be no distinction in pay based on sex," "it is obvious and true that there are certain types of work which can be best performed by men. It is equally true that there are other types of work in which women excel."[13]) Opponents of the ERA cited its possible effects on such issues as custody awards and the military draft. These arguments were also based on biology, claiming that women are naturally better nurturers than men or that women do not have the physical and mental characteristics befitting a soldier.[14]

A number of important challenges have been raised against biological determinism. It has been pointed out, for example, that biological determinism wrongly characterizes the sexes as groups whose members are all alike, that it ignores socialization in treating sexual differences as innate and unchangeable, that appeals to biological differences are often vague, inconsistent across time, bereft of scientific evidence, and blind to the work women have performed across cultures and historical eras.

These challenges, though forceful, do not offer a complete response to biological determinism, for they treat it entirely as a theory about biology and neglect its moral dimensions. To see what antifeminists are up to, look at biological determinism on the micro level. Say that you and your new partner are working out a division of household chores. You are taller than your partner, who in turn is capable of carrying more weight. One could reasonably conclude that because you are taller you should change lightbulbs and paint ceilings, while your stronger partner should move furniture and take out the trash.

What are the advantages of such a scheme? Like the three classes in Plato's *Republic*, everyone has their own tasks, and everyone contributes their best to the whole using their given abilities. The existence of different abilities allows an efficient division of labor where each task is attended to by a person competent to perform it. Lastly, the appeal to preexisting differences establishes a clear criterion by which to decide who does what, solving fundamental problems and skirting arguments.

It may appear that this approach's appeal to biological determinism is one that claims that sex differences *mandate* differential treatment; after all, women are delicate, timid, physically weaker than men, pregnable, and vulnerable to sexual attack. But the language of these opinions is generally not that sure of itself. *Bradwell*, in calling women's "timidity and delicacy" "proper" as well as "natural," seems at least as prescriptive as it is (ostensibly) descriptive. Likewise, *Muller* appeals not only to a woman's "physical structure" but also to "a proper discharge of her maternal functions." That is, a woman's prescribed "proper" social function is assigned *on the basis of* her gender, not *because* of it in some inevitable sense. Once assigned, that function becomes a justification for limitations on women, lest they compromise or injure their capacity to fulfill that function "properly."

Further, *Radice* does not contend that no men are adversely affected by nighttime labor, and it does not see the negative effects on women as only organic but says that it "threatens to impair their peculiar and natural funcions"—those of wife and motherhood. *Muller* says only that certain labor "tends" toward injurious effects on women. In *Dothard*, too, the same weight is given to potential threats and possible tendencies, here called "risks," all of which are to be distinguished from inevitable and universal events.

Thus, what biological determinism looks like in these cases is not always or only an argument that biological, psychological, emotional, and intellectual differences inevitably and profoundly dictate different legal rights and responsibilities. That variety of biological determinism is a relatively easy opponent. But more than an argument about biology is involved. An endorsement of a particular social arrangement is at least as central (more so, I would say), one that gets called "proper" rather than inevitable. If you take biological determinists to be saying biology makes the traditional sexual division of labor preferable, rather than inevitable, you gain entry into their framework of values, issues of why one thing is to be preferred to another. Something is preferable that can offer certain significant advantages not offered by the alternatives or that avoids dangers the alternatives cannot.

The advantages that are seen to flow from the sexual division of labor include the establishment of a system that offers the emotional security of knowing one's role, the social efficiency of specialization, and the philosophical certainty of standards by which one's place is determined. Conversation with biological determinists now leaves the realm of hormones, wombs, and muscles and enters the field of values.

Security, efficiency, and certainty are held to be goods, things worth preserving. This is not blatantly unreasonable, for insecurity can lead to paralyzing fear, inefficiency can cause bad products and wasted time, and uncertainty can bring about error and misdirected wanderings. Such things, it seems, are what antifeminists fear.

In saying that women's proper role is to nurture and support their husbands and children, and men's proper role is to provide for and protect their wives and children, antifeminists are not appealing only or even at all to inevitable biological predispositions or destinies. Instead, what they purport to offer is a division of labor that delineates a clear and socially necessary function for each sex, a role into which each can and must be trained so as to make everyone willing and able to perform their tasks well, for the sake of social order and personal well-being. Thus, feminists who demand equal pay or child care services challenge these roles and thereby the security and efficiency that arise from them. Those supporting the ERA challenge the "noble lie" of innate sex differences on which the entire order rests.

I would like to think it possible to acknowledge both the validity of these concerns and their short-sightedness. If I can indulge in a time-honored male metaphor (being taken over by women's soft-ball!), a critique of antifeminist biological determinism should show that although security, efficiency, and certainty can be posi-tive goods, these values are not the only players on the ballfield, and they are not always the best players. Too much security can cause bravado; too much certainty can cause closed-mindedness, prejudice, and hatred. Too much concern with efficiency may mean some will always sit on the bench, and presently poor but poten-tially good players will not have the opportunity to develop.

The fears, concerns, and values of antifeminists revealed here help establish an agenda for some of the work to be done by femi-nists. Although security can arise from knowing one's place, it needs to be shown that it also comes from having a *good* place and that like stress, a certain amount of insecurity may be beneficial. We need to show, too, that the personal and social costs of some choos-ing "badly" in the absence of traditional sexual guidelines is less than the cost of some being forced into slots into which they do not fit.[15] We may need to develop more argument not only showing that freedom and efficiency are often compatible but exploring the question of when efficiency matters and when it needs to be over-ridden by other values. The antifeminist concern with the clear guidelines offered by the sexual division of labor is important and potent in a society that equips us with few skills for solving or living harmoniously with disagreements or uncertainty. This last theme is one I return to in the third section.

Liberal Capitalism

Liberal theory has often been at the service of feminism, especially in the law. For example, the liberal principle that people must be judged as individuals, not on the basis of their membership in a group, is at the heart of Title VII legislation on equal employment, which has led to tearing down everything from sex-biased job ad-vertising to unequal pension plans.

It may then be a bit surprising to some to discover that a funda-mental assumption of classical liberal theory has also been the enemy of just and progressive legislation for women. A recurrent theme in liberal theory is a vision of a world of limited resources, in which individuals compete for desired goods, trying to maximize their individual self-interest. Historically, the liberal conception of the individual as "economic man," self-interested, calculating, and competitive, has played a pivotal and fascinating role in cases defending sexual differentiation.

To return to the case of *Muller v. Oregon*, in addition to appeals to biological determinism the Court held that protective legislation for women was not only reasonable but necessary because "in the struggle for subsistence she [woman] is not an equal competitor with her brother . . . . [F]rom the viewpoint of the effort to maintain an independent position in life, she is not upon an equality." Now if the woman the Court speaks of here is traditional woman, these statements are unquestionably true. A woman taught to adorn, accommodate, assist, and acquiesce is not likely to be one who is given promotions, power, and privilege. That is, traditional woman is *not* an equal competitor against economic man in a marketplace that honors and rewards aggression, ambition, and avarice.

For liberal feminists the solution to this problem is the creation of "economic woman," who *can* compete and win. But this liberal feminist solution is rejected by liberal capitalist antifeminists, not necessarily on the grounds that women *cannot* be such creatures but because they believe women *ought* not to be. The creation of economic woman, this theory holds, will bring harm to women, their families, and society.

Women, of course, are often held responsible for every "decline" of civilization, every "defect" in their offspring, and every "deviation" by their husbands. Such claims appear too far-fetched to be based on or susceptible to reasoned argument. But court cases can help us unravel the mystery and reveal the antifeminist assumptions and values at work here.

Muller v. Oregon mentions the need "to protect [woman] from the greed . . . of man." *West Coast Hotel v. Parrish*, the 1937 case upholding minimum wage laws for women only, asks, "What can be closer to the public interest than the . . . protection [of women] from unscrupulous and overreaching employers?"[16]

The common thread in these cases is their understanding of the dynamics of life in the public realm. In the *West Coast Hotel* case, the Court stated, "The adoption of similar [minimum wage] requirements by many States evidences a deep-seated conviction both as to the presence of the evil and as to the means adopted to check it." The "evil" about which this "deep-seated conviction" exists concerns life in the marketplace.

Female workers are characterized by the Court as "the ready victims of those who would take advantage of their necessitous circumstances." "Unconscionable employers," the Court said, displaying a "selfish disregard of the public interest," are "unscrupulous" and "overreaching." The Court itself, I should note, had earlier defended the employer against a female minimum wage law.[17] Such a law, it declared, "amounts to a compulsory exaction from the employer for the support of a partially indigent person, for whose condition there rests upon him no peculiar responsibility. . . . The declared basis [of these laws] . . . is the extraneous circumstance that the employee needs to get a prescribed sum of money to insure her subsistence, health and morals."

The recognition of greed and unscrupulousness cited here paints a picture of a public realm that is a jungle-like, dog-eat-dog, look-out-for-number-one world: inhuman, beastlike, machine-like, where even the employee's need for an income ensuring her subsistence and health is considered an "extraneous circumstance." *This* is the evil the Court recognizes.

The means adopted to check this evil, the Court said, is also a matter of deep-seated conviction. The solution is "protective" legislation for women, laws that bar employers from hiring women at certain jobs, hours, or wages. How does the Court understand this to be a reasonable solution? What problems does it solve?

The most obvious answer is that protective legislation shields women from the harsher brutalities of the public world. But more is going on here, aside from concern with women workers. The case of *U.S. v. St. Clair*, holding constitutional a male-only draft, claims that "if a nation is to survive, men must provide the first line of defense while women keep the home fires burning."[18] In 1961, in *Hoyt v. Florida*, the Court upheld voluntary state jury service for women, stating that "it is [not] constitutionally impermissible for a State . . . to conclude that a woman should be relieved from the civic duty of jury service unless she herself determines that such service is consistent with her own special responsibilities."[19]

As it has been portrayed, the marketplace driven by the profit motive, the political arena framed by clashing narrow interests, and the military field laid with violence and hatreds are all contentious places. To survive there participants must be ruthless competitors, ambitious individualists, fierce fighters. These are not necessarily held to be objectively desirable roles, or certainly not the only desirable roles, but someone has to fill them "if a nation is to survive."

In upholding sexual differentiation, the Court is saying that we don't want a world composed entirely of ruthless, fierce individuals. A more humane and loving place must be established and protected to avoid a Hobbesian war of all against all, and to give those who must fight the nasty fight a refuge both to refuel them and to ensure that they are not rendered heartless. Hence, women "keep the home fires burning" to motivate and reward men for their socially necessary labor and to make sure that we don't all become like them, that the world isn't created entirely in their image.

Thus, in opposing liberal feminism's advocacy of "economic woman," what some defenders of difference see themselves as defending is that "haven in a heartless world" found in the traditional family held together by the traditional woman. What they fear is that we will all become heartless, isolated, competitive, and individualistic. Woman's traditional role of nurturing, supporting and bonding people together is a necessary antidote and counterweight.

Four assumptions operate in this theory. First, that human nature being what it is, the public realm *must* be modeled on economic man; second, that the creation of public workers and warriors requires creation of motivating and compensating forces, which can be found in the private realm; third, that the one who competes all day cannot be the one responsible for establishing a place grounded in nurture, care, and respect (even though this person desires and to some extent participates in it); and fourth, that to take support away from the private haven is to create a hellish world.

The argument that follows from these assumptions, to return to the cases cited earlier, is that (a) woman needs to be protected from the greed that reigns in the marketplace *in order* to perform "her own special responsibilities" and to "keep the home fires burning," and (b) woman *must* keep the home fires burning for important *political* reasons: first, to reward and motivate men; second, to prevent the war of all against all.

The importance of maintaining a realm that is immune to the dynamics of the public world is also obvious in opposition to the 1971 Child Advocacy Act. First, concern with "put[ting] government in the place of the parent"[20] is in part a concern with keeping some arena clear of the influence of the "expert," bureaucratic mode of doing business. The private and personal are seen as "communalized," taken over by the government; hence, the complementary function of the family (identical with the family in this debate) is "destroyed." Accordingly, children will become an "industry" and suffer "the disease of non-attachment."[21]

At least some opposition to the ERA was resistance to the idea of women as primary or equal wage earners, an economic role understood as incompatible with nurture and support of men and children. Likewise, the ERA was seen as encouraging women to enter the public arena and as dangerously ignoring and devaluing the importance of women's traditional role.

Antifeminists' rejection of feminism comes in part because they see the whole of feminism as liberal feminism at its worst—that is, feminism that urges women to be like men.[22] This they fear, as do many nonliberal feminists. There is a level at which some antifeminists value women's traditional morality and way of being in the world, sometimes almost displaying a hunger for it. They don't think you can have it everywhere, but they mourn the possibility of having it nowhere. The liberal feminist argument that women should become the independent, self-interested, rational contractors that men are, in politics, at work, and in the home, only expands the number of people who become morally impoverished and extends the domain in which the morality of "economic man" reigns. Antifeminist refusal to endorse this has a laudable dimension, even if it is ultimately misdirected.

Thus seen, nonliberal feminists and antifeminists actually share

certain assumptions: that the world of paid labor, as currently constructed on the profit motive, hurts us as individuals and fosters
traits that are socially undesirable and that the family, even as it is
currently constructed, at least sometimes offers something better.
Both sides are saying this, a fact I see as overlooked.

Feminists' solutions to this problem differ from those of the antifeminists because the latter assume that it *must* be a jungle out
there, dystopian as it is, and that it is always peaceful and loving in
the home. They fail to consider seriously whether inhumane treatment of wage laborers is necessary or even ultimately profitable or
to ask who is and is not getting nurtured in the home that must
now by definition be seen as at the service of the public realm. By
structuring the private realm almost entirely with an eye to its political functions, antifeminists remain aloof from its other dimensions.

The agenda for feminism that emerges from this discussion of
liberal capitalist antifeminism is to pay more attention to how various forms of the family can be compatible with both feminist ideals
and social requirements. In recognizing the economic, political, and
moral importance of the family, antifeminists may be right in sus-
pecting some feminists of being too glib. If the family does have
important political consequences, then liberal feminist talk about
one arrangement being as good as any other, without assurances of
their positive contribution to politics, personal relationships, and
child development, may be less mysteriously and more under-
standably suspect.

Psychological Pessimism

In discussing biological determinism earlier, I noted the antifeminist concern with emotional security and certainty of standards.
The desire for moral clarity, simplicity, and uniformity is also
shown in family law cases and gives voice to what I am calling
antifeminist moral and psychological pessimism.

The ex-husband of a woman cohabitating with another man sued
for custody of the children on the ground that they were endangered by her conduct. The Illinois Supreme Court in 1979 granted

him custody.[23] The court appealed in part to the fact that "psychological effects or problems may later develop from [the children's] efforts to overcome the disparity between their concepts of propriety and their mother's conduct. . . . [If one] contravene[s] statutorily declared standards of conduct, [it will] endanger the children's moral development." In cases involving lesbian mothers, women have lost custody of their children because a lover sometimes stayed in the home,[24] because of a commitment to a lesbian relationship,[25] and because of violation of a court order to keep her lesbian lover from contact with her children.[26] In each of these cases simple exposure to a lesbian environment was held to cause sufficient harm to children to justify loss of custody. Lastly, in a Supreme Court case denying the father of an "illegitimate" child the right to sue for the child's wrongful death, Justice Stewart wrote that it is "neither illogical nor unjust for society to express its 'condemnation of irresponsible liaisons beyond the bounds of marriage' by not conferring" such rights to the biological father.[27]

These cases argue that the traditional family is best for children and that legal penalties on nontraditional families are logical and just. What exactly do the courts here see themselves as defending and protecting? In stating that children are morally damaged by living in a household that challenges social standards of conduct, the courts are hoping to present children with an environment that provides clear and consistent rules of moral conduct and that protects them from peer ridicule or harassment. In calling a disparity between socially dominant standards of conduct and the conduct within a child's household psychologically and morally damaging, the court is assuming that psychological health and development of the human sense of propriety are dependent on the presence of a uniform standard of conduct. Human morality is seen as so fragile that the existence of diverse models potentially has the same harmful consequences as no standards. And, in denying certain rights to unmarried fathers on the grounds that doing so discourages "irresponsible liaisons," the courts seem to be saying that left to themselves, without an official state system of rewards and punishments for certain behaviors, people will often act irresponsibly.

In opposition to feminist legislation, the concern with providing

people with the motivation to act in a way compatible with fulfillment of social and moral responsibilities, and to prevent the establishment of incentives that would encourage them to do otherwise,
is truly a dominant theme. What comes through is less a concern
with the moral, social, or legal *rights* of individuals than with their
moral, social, and legal *responsibilities*. The assumption is that society has the need and right to make men and women fulfill certain
roles, roles that presumably they might otherwise shun, at great
peril.

In letters and articles included in the *Congressional Record*, the
1971 Child Advocacy Act was called a challenge to "our faith in
. . . individual responsibility." The fear was that the bill would be
"relieving mothers of the responsibility of raising their children."
"Even mothers who don't need to work can take advantage of the
State training so as to release them for other things." Other articles
said groups like "Women's Lib" were advocating the bill "to free
them from the restrictive life of small children at home" and might
"reduce the family's feelings of responsibility."

One analysis of anti-ERA forces argues that in blurring the clear
distinction between the roles of women and men, the ERA, opponents feared, would cause a dimunition in the motivation of both
sexes to carry out socially necessary tasks. For example, if men used
to be willing to wage war because that was the duty of male citizens
(in large part in defense of women and children), then removing
that link between sex and social duties may make it no one's clear
responsibility or may remove what has served as sufficient motivation.

The assumptions that there is a human propensity to immorality
and that the fewer the models of acceptable moral behavior, the
greater the chances of conformity and security, help explain antifeminist rejection of feminism's insistence on choice and diversity.
Antifeminists' clamoring for a return to traditional values seems to
arise from an almost Hobbesian belief that the only two alternatives
are a single model of moral behavior and moral anarchy.

Evidence for a human propensity to immorality and irresponsi-
bility, or for the notion that diversity is dangerously baffling, is not
offered. But it probably is correct to say that in general antifemi-

nism does provide a world view with clear guidelines. Antifeminism tells us with a scary certainty everything from who should call whom for a date and who should do what tasks in the household, to what relationships and positions constitute sexual morality. The antifeminist fear might be directed at such once-famous sayings as "If it feels good, do it" and "Do your own thing."

It is worth noting that this aspect of antifeminism, unlike others, does *not* see procreation, heterosexuality, or sexual hierarchy as occurring naturally—that is, without social enforcement. But the sort of security offered by antifeminism is not simply to be sneezed at. Especially in the contemporary world, where philosophers from Rousseau to Marx have commented on the awesome pace of change, having something to hold on to may enable one to hold on. Further, in a world dominated more and more by ideologies of self-interest, the antifeminist concern with obligations to others is not unwelcome.

In responding to antifeminism arising from moral pessimism, feminists may find it useful to emphasize the centrality of our concern with morality and to work on clarifying our conceptions of moral possibilities. For example, condemnation of rape, family violence, and pornography are rooted in notions of how people ought to view and treat each other. Advocacy of equal pay and comparable worth are based on obligations of decency and fairness. Pro-abortion feminists reaffirm concern with the quality of life and the value of autonomy. Feminism teems with values that are laudable, from respect and nonviolence to autonomy and equity. In fact, feminists condemn the antifeminist status quo precisely on the basis of *its* immorality, for which evidence is all to easy to pile up.

Antifeminist concern with moral security is ultimately shallow, for it rests content with superficial conformity, calculates the benefits of security without counting the uncompensable costs to those for whom the model of morality is oppressive or destructive, and assumes that one model of familial morality answers all of the most important moral questions and thus provides security and certainty.

Feminism does not hold that all people are automatically decent—just look around—but perhaps holds more hope that people can create a culture that encourages them to be truly decent, a hope that could benefit from more theoretical and practical backing. And, finally, feminism seems more willing to live with the risks, uncertainties, and complexities that are part of life than are antifeminists, who do theory like I keep house, sweeping the dust under the carpet and hoping nobody looks around too carefully.

Conclusion

I have tried to show two things in this essay. First, that just as feminism is not reducible to a single theory, neither is antifeminism; that is, all antifeminists are not alike. Especially important here is the realization that not all antifeminist arguments rely on assumptions about biological differences but appeal to political, psychological, moral, and economic concerns. Second, a more careful look at antifeminist theories and concerns helps point out some issues that feminists would do well to address with more insight and precision. Antifeminists are not all simply evil, disdainful of women, or ignorant. They at least sometimes give voice to important concerns about human relationships, security, and social well-being. Clarifying what they are for and against may enable a better dialogue between the two sides that can result in a future that is soundly feminist. Phyllis Schlafly and Jerry Falwell still may not rush to sign up, but we make them less credible witnesses when we understand their concerns and meet them head-on with better answers.

Notes

1. Rebecca Klatch, in *Women of the New Right* (Philadelphia: Temple University Press, 1987), asks a similar question: "How do women of the New Right look at the world?" (4). Her inquiry, however, is both broader and narrower than mine: broader, in that she is interested in "right-wing women," whom she argues are not all antifeminist; narrower, in that she is interested only in "right-wing women," not all opponents of feminism.

2. Discussing the emphasis on suffrage in the women's movement from 1848 to 1920, Eileen Kraditor notes, "The chance to change these

[discriminatory] laws was a powerful incentive for suffragism." *Up from the Pedestal: Selected Writing in the History of American Feminism* (Chicago: Quadrangle Books, 1968), 18.

3. Leo Kanowitz, *Women and the Law: The Unfinished Revolution* (Albuquerque: University of New Mexico Press, 1969), 1.

4. Alexis de Tocqueville, *Democracy in America* (Garden City, N.Y.: Anchor Books, 1969), 270.

5. *Bradwell v. Illinois* 83 U.S. (16 Wall.) 130, emphasis added.

6. *Muller v. Oregon*, 208 U.S. 412, emphasis added.

7. *Radice v. New York*, 264 U.S. 292, emphasis added.

8. *Dothard v. Rawlinson*, 433 U.S. 321, emphasis added.

9. *Michael M. v. Sonoma County*, 450 U.S. 464, emphasis added.

10. Willis Tucker, "News and Comment," *Western Sun* (Everett, Wash.), October 1, 1971. Cited in the *Congressional Record*, November 16, 1971, p. 41598.

11. Iowans for Moral Education, "Whose Children? Yours or the States'?" Included in the *Congressional Record-House*, November 16, 1971, p. 41596.

12. Representative Findley, *Congressional Record-House*, May 23, 1963, p. 9205.

13. Representative Cohelan (Oklahoma), *Congressional Record-House*, May 23, 1962, p. 9212.

14. In *Why We Lost the ERA* (Chicago: University of Chicago Press, 1986), Jane Mansbridge lists these as two of the issues that anti-ERA forces considered important and representative.

15. In an article that does try to understand the values of antifeminists, Joyce Trebilcot leaves this challenge unanswered, simply pointing out that antifeminists have not proved that the cost of choosing badly is greater than the cost of not being able to choose. This is logically correct but does not make much progress in the argument. "Sex Roles: The Argument from Nature," *Ethics* 85 (1975), 249–55.

16. *West Coast Hotel v. Parrish*, 300 U.S. 379.

17. *Adkins v. Children's Hospital*, 261 U.S. 525, 1923.

18. *U.S. v. St. Clair*, 291 F.Supp. 122.

19. *Hoyt v. Florida*, 368 U.S. 57.

20. "Legislative Emergency Memo," Cincinnati, Ohio, included in the *Congressional Record-House* by Representative Rarick, November 16, 1971, p. 41594.

21. The Joint Commission on Mental Health of Children was accused in the *Record* of calling children an industry. Konrad Lorenz was given credit for connecting institutional child care with "nonattachment" and was frequently cited in the debates.

22. One useful example of this, and there are many, is Robert E. Gould's

"Why Can't a (Working) Woman Be More Like a Man?" *Working Woman*, April 1985.

23. *Jarrett v. Jarrett*, 78 Ill.2d 337, 400 N.E.2d 421, 36 (Ill. Dec. 1).

24. *Mueller v. Mueller*, No. 79 DR 1246 (Colo. Ct. App., Nov. 19, 1981).

25. *Hall v. Hall*, 95 Mich. App. 614, 291 N.W. 2d 143 (1980).

26. *N.K.M. v. L.E.M.*, 606 S.W. 2d 179 (Mo. Ct. App. 1980).

27. *Parham v. Hughes*, 99 S.Ct. 1742.

Plato's **Republic** *I as Male Dialogue*

I wrote this piece after a particularly disastrous semester teaching Plato's Republic. *Here was a book that had first attracted me to political theory as an undergraduate student, and now I dreaded having to read it again and talk about it for weeks on end. I was unsure what had happened. Writing at the end of the semester, it became clear to me that the text was incredibly male and that the maleness was what I was now responding to so negatively. This essay is my attempt to show, through an examination of Book I, what is so male about it. The essay is in part a conversation between me and defenders of Plato's "feminism." But it is primarily about silencing—the absence of dialogue.*

> For it matters to us what is said about us, who says it, and to whom it is said: having the opportunity to talk about one's life, to give an account of it, to interpret it, is integral to leading that life rather than being led through it . . . To put the same point slightly differently, part of human life, human living, is talking about it, and we can be sure that being silenced in one's own account of one's life is a kind of amputation that signals oppression.
>
> Maria Lugones and Elizabeth Spelman,
> "Have We Got a Theory for You!"

4

¢ ¢ ¢

Plato's *Republic* I as Male Dialogue: A Case Study of Gender Exclusivity in Political Theory

> The fact that no woman participates in any of the [Platonic] dialogues in person merely constitutes evidence of the prevailing attitudes of the time and the characteristics of Athenian life they produced. . . . [It] says nothing about Plato except that he chose to set his dialogues realistically in the context of contemporary society.[1]

W omen's absence in Platonic dialogues does indeed reflect the dominant attitudes of fifth-century B.C.E. Athens. Secluded domesticity was a common fate of Athenian women. Access to the public arena was virtually forbidden to them, and their education was minimal, a fact not unrelated to the young age at which they were married[2] and at which they died.[3] Educationally, religiously, socially, and politically, women were neither prepared nor permitted to live the kind of lives participation in the dialogues presumed and required.[4]

Nonetheless, the absence of female participants in the dialogues[5] does much more than offer objective evidence of ancient Athenian mores. It allows the discussions to slight, misrepresent, or altogether omit mention of women's experiences, relationships, concerns, values, and questions. Pinpointing the *source* of women's exclusion in patriarchal Athenian culture does nothing to mitigate the *effects* of women's absence on the substance of the dialogues. Ultimately, the effect is to consign women's lives to the margins of philosophy and politics, while certain male experiences and values establish the boundaries of the fields and define the substance of the enterprises.

Especially since the early 1970s, debates over Plato's "feminism," or lack thereof, have focused largely on such issues as Plato's motives in granting women and men equal opportunity to become philosopher-rulers, the extent to which he believed women (individually and as a class) to be men's equals, the consistency of his views on women in various works, and the meaning and implications of negative, stereotypical characterizations of women found throughout his writings.[6] Studying these issues has generally involved measuring passages against one another in the search for a clear and consistent message. But the debate over Plato's "feminism" most emphatically should not focus exclusively on his scattered statements explicitly about women. Such a focus not only runs interpretive risks by removing comments from their individual contexts but, more important for purposes here, also does injustice to feminism by defining it much too narrowly, turning a wide-ranging political philosophy into a checklist or a narrow status report.

I propose a different strategy by which to evaluate Plato[7] from a feminist perspective, one that does not even use his comments specifically about sexual (in)equality. I will argue that Plato's *Republic* I is a quintessentially masculine, or patriarchal, text because the dialogue portrays a world inhabited in important ways only by free men, with its examples, questions, and answers being based on those Greek male experiences. Women's experiences and values are all too frequently absent from or peripheral in his dialogues and theories.[8] Women's distinct voices, borne from lives different from men's at almost every juncture, are noticeably silenced in discussion of issues both related and seemingly unrelated to gender. Certainly anyone with a claim to the title of "feminist" would not search for "knowledge" omitting half of the radically gender-differentiated human experiences of their time and would see such differentiation itself as an important political and philosophical issue.

In this study of the first book of the *Republic*,[9] I discuss how the setting, questions, reactions, and answers of each scene reflect and present male perspectives and experiences and how, consequently, Athenian women's lives are unrepresented, rendered invisible and philosophically irrelevant. My intent is to reveal the patriarchal undertow that silently and forcefully directs the flow of conversation into certain channels and away from others, as well as to explore some of the repercussions of this diversion. I also show some of what is omitted from or invisible in Plato by noting the different questions women's lives might have given rise to, had they been at all considered in the dialogue.

My greatest frustration in writing this essay arose from an attempt to actually rewrite the dialogue, this time including among the participants several women. I could not find the words or the tone that Athenian women from different classes, of different ages, and with different sexual identities might have used. There were many differences between women, as one might expect in such a patriarchal and hierarchicalized culture. Hetaerae, "companions" (but not wives) to upper-class Athenian males, were the most educated women, the sort of "exceptional" women Plato knew (as he did Aspasia) and might have had in mind as he wrote of philosopher-queens; concubines, generally poor prostitutes who were widows, slaves, and girls abandoned as infants, we know little about; "free" wives, or citizen women, the blood relatives of male citizens, were workhorses of sorts and the most secluded and restricted women; poor women may have had more freedom of movement than "highborn" citizen women and were frequently employed (as women still are today) doing for others what they also did in their own homes, as washerwomen and nursemaids, for example. "Athenian law, like that of most Greek communities, made very clear the differences between the various groups of women; there were citizen women and metic women (resident non-citizens from another *polis*); there were upper-class women and lower-class women.''[10] Though not a trouble-free solution, the compromise I ended up with is to use the voice of the U.S., white, educated, middle-class feminist I am to give voice, with some historical accuracy, to issues raised by the different lives various Athenian women then led and to keep in sight the fact that ''whichever group they belonged to, [women] all had one thing in common: they had no political rights of any kind. At every stage in their lives they were under the control of men,''[11] and distinctions between groups of women were frequently based on their relationships to distinctive groups of men. There is little assurance in this compromise that Athenian women would have raised similar issues in similar ways; this uncertainty is itself a consequence of women's absence in philosophical texts!

Book I can be rather neatly divided into four sections, each of which I will discuss in turn.

1. (327a–328b) The opening scene. A group of men, led by Polemarchus, induce Glaucon and Socrates, all of whom are leaving a festival, to join them.
2. (328b–331d) The group arrives at Polemachus' house, where a gathering of men already exists, including Cephalus, Polemarchus' father. Cephalus and Socrates briefly discuss the pros and cons of growing old, the advantages of wealth, and justice as law-abidingness.
3. (331e–336a) Polemarchus proposes a second definition of justice, as benefiting friends and harming enemies. Discussion ensues.
4. (336b–354c) Thrasymachus angrily asserts that justice is nothing but the advantage of the stronger. Discussion ensues.

Scene I: The Persuasion

Polemarchus and his friends do not want Socrates and Glaucon to return to the city after the festival at the Piraeus celebrating the Thracian goddess Bentis. Polemarchus' ''slave boy'' catches up with them and relates that ''Polemarchus orders you to wait'' (327b).[12]

"Guessing" that they "are hurrying to get away to town," Polemarchus says, "Do you see how many of us there are? . . .[E]ither prove stronger than these men, or stay here" (327c). Socrates asks whether he and Glaucon may persuade the others to let them go, but Polemarchus informs him that those who do not listen cannot possibly be persuaded, and they have no intention of listening (327c). Adeimantus and Polemarchus then entice Socrates and Glaucon to stay with the promise of a novel "torch race on horseback" (which, incidentally, they never see), an "all-night festival," "dinner," and the company of "many of the young men" to talk with (328a). At this point Glaucon and Socrates agree, "It seems we must stay" (328b).

This opening scene sets the stage well for a male dialogue, for it is replete with strategies and responses available only to privileged men and identified strongly with them. That is, the parties are able to act and speak as they do because they are free and male, and in so acting and speaking they are displaying behavior appropriate to their gender and class.

A. The Setting

The setting itself is a masculine one, for it is not clear that women would even have been attending the festival in the first place, and especially not the later gathering at Polemarchus' home. No women were allowed at Olympia (and male slaves were not allowed to be spectators) and likely not at other Panhellenic festivals either. At those special festivals of their own country that women and men could attend, women were segregated and generally limited to certain duties assigned to them by men—practices of exclusion and separation that "express the male sense that the very threat posed by what is female should be contained."[13] The very infrequency of women's participation in a festival, all-female or otherwise, as in anything outside the confines of the *gynoeconitis*, or women's rooms, may well have made the experience quite different from what it was for men. Some think even female friendships were suspect at the time among citizen women: "the gathering of women was discouraged by the husbands, who believed the effect of gossip to be matrimonial discontent." To say the least, opportunities for social life were not abundant.

Greek women "saw few men besides their husbands: the social gatherings of the Greeks were as masculine as the rest of their lives."[14]

> It was of such overriding importance not to allow the least breath of suspicion to fall on young girls that they were not virgins, or on young wives that their child was not properly conceived in wedlock, that they were protected [*sic*] to . . . a wholly unreasonable degree. . . . Other speakers claim that wives do not go out to dinner with their husbands, and do not even eat with their husbands when they are entertaining male visitors, unless they are relatives. . . . It is to be remembered that since gay parties and serenadings were regarded as the mark of a kept woman, this provided yet another reason for a wife not to wish to attend.[15]

Even commentators who note the exclusively male setting do not elaborate on or mention any consequences of it. But imagine a philosophical dialogue today being held in an all-male club (i.e., a fraternity house, a professional men's organization) after some ritual controlled and staged largely by and for men (i.e., a football game, a "strip show"). Surely some suspicion that the exclusive company and charged atmosphere affected the substance of the conversation would be warranted. And relations among privileged Athenian men were highly charged, both by "the competitiveness, envy, and distrust intrinsic to the contest system" and by the sexual relations among them that occurred in the context of that contest system.[16]

Despite the fact that those at Polemarchus' house were young and old, citizen and alien resident, all were male, and this feature of the setting does have significant consequences. As is the case in all-male militaries, fraternities, and sports teams, part of what happens in bringing only men together is that some of the glue bonding them as a community is made up of their differences from and social superiority over women. Even conversational dynamics change when only men are present, adopting a more competitive form. And a purpose and consequence of these male-controlled events is to protect privileges through exclusivity and internal networks. From the opening scene we are situated in no-woman's land.

B. Relations between the Free and Enslaved

It is only as a free man that Polemarchus issues "orders," through "his slave boy," to Socrates and Glaucon. Obedience to men is a central part of the definition of virtue for Greek women and enslaved Greek men; their function is to receive and heed orders rather than issue them, whereas to be free and male is to do the reverse.

"Free" women's relations with slaves may have been quite different from those between free and enslaved men. "Free" women, for example, often worked alongside the female slaves on many of the same tasks and shared the political status of outsider. We do not know if habituation to male power made citizen women's exercise of power over the enslaved different from that exercised by men. And perhaps because enslaved men were paid more than their female counterparts, leaving males with a greater chance of buying their freedom, the presumed permanency of the relationship between citizen women and enslaved women may also have marked it as distinctive from those between men. Portrayals of these female relationships are nonexistent in the *Republic*, blessing male relationships with an unwarranted presumption of representativeness and normalcy.[17]

C. Force

If Greek women were the characters here, it is unlikely that the book would open with a threat of physical force, backed up, in addition, by all "these men" who are allies through either male friendship or a relationship of subservience. It would be surprising if using or threatening to use brute force was commonplace among women who were virtually confined to the household, had received little physical training, and had been taught to obey. Enslaved women might be physically stronger from being assigned more manual labor, but their status as slaves would compromise their ability to rally others to support their position in a fight and would make it dangerous to threaten others above them in Athenian hierarchies. By contrast, it seems that free Greek boys of all economic classes received training in wrestling, boxing, running, jumping, and throwing the discus and spear. In addition, boys of aristocratic families were trained in the use of arms and in military tactics.[18]

Socrates' request that he and Glaucon have the opportunity to persuade the others to let them go reflects his male privilege of being able to speak directly (whereas women are more confined to indirect forms of persuasion) and his access as a male to practice in the logical and rhetorical skills necessary to attempt such a persuasion. Women's education, like men's, prepared them for their social destiny. But since women's position involved subordination to men and confinement to domestic tasks, Athenian girls of all economic classes were ill educated.

Members of oppressed groups have more access to indirect forms of persuasion than direct. They may be punished for direct challenges and requests and accepted more when they speak and act in such a way as to present no perceived threat—timidly, through insinuation, or without taking credit for their ideas. Further, subordinated people know too well the futility and danger of directly challenging those who will not listen and who have explicitly marked the issue as a contentious one. Appeals to force may rightly be countered with Socratic persuasion, but appeals formally and substantively based on the narrower options available within a given context may do so as well. That is, women's forms of persuasion and wisdom often differ greatly from those of men in sexually differentiated societies, and the *Republic* allows readers to neglect or disparage the former without cause.

The opening scene does reveal certain dynamics and consequences of an imbalance of power. The scene could be used to discuss how, with institutionalized inequality, might is often appealed to as a matter of course, not as a last resort but as a first one. It is also often the only response that is listened to. (The only alternative to staying proposed by the "gentlemen" is winning a physical fight while outnumbered.) Similarly, the scene assumes a conflict of interests before establishing that there is one, for although Socrates and Glaucon may have been heading back to the city, there is no evidence that it was something on which their hearts were firmly set.[19] It is those who are sure of their dominance who have the right and the might to force and win a fight. Further, the empowered never directly state that they simply want the company of Glaucon and Socrates but insist at the outset that the latter should stay without first respectfully having or desiring to say why. And those in power often make their demands, as Polemarchus does, assuming that the other has no conflicting obligations. Charlotte Perkins Gilman noted this last phenomenon as characteristic of women's fate where women are economically dependent on men:

> Another discord introduced by the condition of servitude is that between will and action. A servant places his time and strength at the disposal of another will. He must hold himself in readiness to do what he is told.[20]

Finally, the scene reveals what women, like members of other, sometimes overlapping oppressed groups, experience regularly: relative powerlessness against those with might, who are willing to use force, even before it is established that a conflict exists or that no other means can resolve it. It is a position that leaves one defensive, vulnerable, distrustful, and fearful. It also often leaves one no better option than seeming to consent, a supposed consent that is then used as evidence of voluntariness, of freedom—of the lack of need for change.

Thus, the setting, dynamics, style, and substance of speech in the opening scene are only appropriate to free men and do not reflect universal human experience or even the experience of any but a minority of fifth-century B.C.E. Athenians. The first scene closes largely as it opened, with reference to the promised company of more men and more festivities at which only men will be in attendance.

Women might have talked to each other differently, and about different matters. Their lives certainly give rise to a separate list of issues. Perhaps they would have discussed the contrast between their normal isolation and their attendance at the festival, raising issues of who counts in what communities and how those communities are sustained. Maybe conversation would have touched on the festival's worship of the new goddess, leading to talk about the "masculine" characters of goddesses (like Athena, often portrayed in statues as a warrior), or about the irony of goddess worship in a culture that ordinarily disdains mortal women. In any event, it is interesting to ponder what directions the dialogue may have gone in, and in what tone, if women were participants. What dangerous truths might have been revealed if women's lives and issues were treated as relevant to politics?

Scene II: Cephalus

Having successfully "persuaded" Socrates and Glaucon to accompany them, the entourage proceeds to Polemarchus' house. The next conversation is between Socrates and Cephalus, Polemarchus' aging father. In a few short passages the two offer reflections on growing old, wealth, and justice. On each subject the views put forth by Cephalus reflect the experiences and opinions of privileged men, and Socrates' challenges to Cephalus do not venture too far from that realm.

Cephalus notes that most bemoan old age, "longing for the pleasures of youth and reminiscing about sex, about drinking bouts and feasts. . . . Some also bewail the abuse that old age receives from relatives" (329a–b). But Cephalus, quoting Sophocles in part, argues that old age brings "escape . . . from a sort of frenzied and savage master . . . [G]reat peace and freedom . . . When the desires cease to strain . . . it is possible to be rid of very many mad masters" (329c–d).

Socrates next asks whether it isn't money more than a moderate disposition that makes Cephalus' old age so endurable, but the latter insists that a bad man, even with money, is not at peace. Socrates attributes Cephalus' moderation about money to the fact that it was mostly inherited, not acquired by his own efforts, to which Cephalus largely agrees. Asked about the greatest benefit of wealth, Cephalus reports that it is "[n]ot to have lied to or deceived anyone even unwillingly, not to depart yonder in fear, owing either sacrifices to a god or money to a man: to this wealth makes a great contribution" (331b). Socrates asks whether this response, which he restates as speaking the truth and paying back debts, amounts to justice, and Cephalus agrees this is not always the case. He then makes his exit to offer a sacrifice, leaving his son Polemarchus, his "heir" (331d), to inherit his argument.

A. "Sex, Drink and Feasts"

Cephalus' explanation of why most bemoan old age refers only to male experiences. The pleasures of "sex, drink and feasts" were available primarily to Greek males and perhaps to a small number of "kept" women. As already noted, Greek citizen women rarely participated in feasts and festivities, and acts of premarital and extramarital sex were among the worst crimes a woman could commit, acts with grave repercussions. Further, enslaved women were subjected to the sexual aggression of the household patriarchs, and poor women could be forced into prostitution.

Whether, like Cephalus' friends, men unambivalently lament their lost youth or, like Cephalus, look back on it as full of too-frenzied desires, the perspectives of both are male. The dialogue is silent, for example, about what it is like to be sent off or sold as teenagers to older husbands their fathers chose, with whom they are not even acquainted, destined for a life of seclusion and domestic service. It is not clear what household abuses women were ever free from or what frenzied desires were ever allowed mastery in their young lives.

B. "Growing Old"

Growing old means different things for men and women in sexually differentiated societies. Continued responsibility for domestic labor, an end to childbearing, changes in child rearing duties, and additional tasks associated with caring for an aging husband may have been more definitive of aging for many Athenian women than would be the loss of the capacity to overindulge in food, liquor, and sex. But such experiences are entirely excluded from the dialogue.

The conversation on aging would certainly be different without the male norm. It would have to take into account that in Greek society then, as in ours, even older women were legally minors, people who never "came of age," under the guardianship of the male to whose household they belonged.

Cephalus' role in the dialogue is problematic on a more symbolic level, too. The only one of his generation present, he represents ancestral rule, the rule of the fathers, tradition. His exit merely replaces the rule of the father with the rule of the son, and it does not challenge masculine right, a failure that compromises the dialogue to come. Ideas and practices of paternal order are left unquestioned. These uncritically accepted opinions will obscure the search for an understanding of justice based on something higher than opinion. As representative of ancestral rule, Cephalus' presence, like women's absence, captures a certain historical reality. And like women's absence, Cephalus' presence has consequences beyond that reality.

C. Wealth

The discussion of wealth is as gendered as the earlier talk on aging. Left out of the dialogue completely is the economic condition of Greek women, who could not own property at all, though they could "inherit" it as a means of transmitting it to another male—a status that marked women as incapable. In fact, "a female heiress . . . was *obliged* to marry her oldest male relative on her father's side so that the property might remain within the family."[21] Talk of women's conditions as they relate to money would also have to confront the practice of dowry, the giving of money to a new husband, the selling of a woman to a husband who will control her.

Although Socrates establishes a meaningful distinction between inherited and acquired wealth, money that women "have" by virtue of attachment to—or, more accurately, belonging to—a male does not fit neatly into either category. Money of one's own, however acquired, may contribute to the truthfulness and peacefulness of Greek men, but the contributors to women's truthfulness, peace-fulness, and justice, and the ramifications of women's particular economic condition, remain a mystery to us after this discussion. How might women's presence have affected this part of the dia-logue? Perhaps by bringing the conversation to the topics of familial duties over the life span, the role of old women as opposed to old men, the continued caretaking functions of poor and enslaved old women, the costs of economic dependence, or the property status of certain human beings. Their presence may have slowed down or derailed Socrates and company's hurried grabbing for universal truths, a quest that, in the *Republic,* is based on too little and system-atically slanted information.

Scene III: Polemarchus

Whereas the conversation between Socrates and Cephalus touched briefly on a number of subjects, that between Socrates and Polemar-chus focuses entirely on unpacking the meaning of Polemarchus' proposed definition of justice: giving each what is owed and fitting them, benefit to friends and harm to enemies. Through Socrates' controlling questions about what "owed" means and about the acts and people to which the "art" of justice pertains, they agree that justice means doing good to friends who are good, but they cannot conclude that it is just to harm even enemies who are bad.

A. Analogies

In the process of trying to discover what situations and people justice applies to, Socrates offers analogies with numerous other arts, including medicine, cooking, sailing, farming, shoe making, draught playing, and house building. It is noteworthy that virtually all of the crafts mentioned here are ones practiced by men.[22] The possible significance of this is threefold.

First, as current debates over standardized intelligence testing continue to show, the constant use of examples that are more famil-iar to men than to women, or to white people than to people of color, has the effect of making a discourse exclusionary. It becomes difficult for some to follow whereas the others, the insiders, effortlessly nod at familiar stories and grasp what they are to take from them. A related effect is that understanding such stories is equated with intelligence, whereas acquaintance with other stories means nothing at best and, at worst, marks one (as one's stories) as trivial and inferior.

Second, it is not clear what the use of other stories and analogies might show. What if, for example, instead of seeking a definition of the art of justice analogous to medicine and sailing, we looked to the art of mothering in Athens? Perhaps the discussants could be led to a definition less "scientific" and universalizable, for as children are both individuals and ever changing, what we owe them must somehow be tailored to them and evolve over time. The inclusion of women's lives even as examples in philosophical argument could alter the course of the conversation.

Third, the analogies are understood as uncritically as they are effortlessly. The popular (male) interpretation is untouched. For example, when Polemarchus asserts, as an example of giving what is owed and fitting, that the art of cooking gives seasonings to meats, he is unchallenged. But the poor might look at the art of cooking as getting the most nutritious and palatable foods out of the most meager of resources, a vegetarian might consider the cooking of meats as not giving to animals what is owed them, and most women could question the connection between such cooking and their assigned role in preparation and their alloted portion. Because the conversation in the *Republic* takes place in the presence of free men who share certain patriarchal understandings, many issues never get raised, yet further arguments are built on these unchallenged assumptions.

B. Harming Enemies

Socrates' female companions would most likely not have made primary the aspect of Polemarchus' definition to which Socrates subsequently objects: harming one's enemies. For reasons stated earlier, women did not have much direct acquaintance with war and aggression but were taught obedience, compromise, and accommodation. Polemarchus equates too much of political life with conflict, exclusivity, and violence. This may be more a statement about the actions and values of patriarchy than about justice, though it is confused for the latter, with a disturbing lack of discomfort.[23] Perhaps this element of harming enemies, however, makes the dialogue in and about the *Republic* so unwelcomingly male. For as Charlotte Perkins Gilman noted in 1923:

> All these stories of adventure, of struggle and difficulty, of hunting and fishing and fighting, of robbing and murdering, catching and punishing, are distinctly and essentially masculine. . . . [Women's] major processes are not those of conflict and adventure, their love means more than mating.[24]

Female companions might have questioned the categories used in the male dialogue from perspectives previously unrepresented. They might have questioned whether the drive to name enemies so preoccupies us that we fail to study and act on what our friends need and deserve. The link between (not) helping friends and harming enemies would be pursued differently. Women's experiences with deprivation and subordination immediately challenge both Athenian practice and ordinary ideas about justice. They might display great interest in deglorifying conquest, a position and virtue not uncommon among the conquered.

Scene IV: Thrasymachus

Thrasymachus, the "wild beast" (336b), appears to be the most stereotypically male character in the dialogue. An orator, he offensively enters the conversation with demands, insults, and accusations, virtually calling Socrates a "wimp" and challenging him to prove his manhood. His scornful outburst leaves the others "afraid," "startled," and "trembling" (336d–e). He desires not only a fee for teaching about justice but also admiration and gratefulness (337d–338b).

Thrasymachus declares, "[T]he just is nothing other than the advantage of the stronger" (338c), and he is "disgusted" (338d) at having to explain himself. His view is that in all regimes the "ruling group sets down laws for its own advantage" and punishes subjects who transgress as lawless and unjust (338e). Thus, what is called just is in fact that which serves those with power. After an argument over the fallibility of rulers, Socrates argues by analogy that every expert seeks the advantage of "what is ruled" (342e), not their own advantage. Thrasymachus continues to argue "that justice and the just are really someone else's good" (343c); those who obey "just" laws are harmed but obey because they are afraid of suffering more injustice if they are caught or if they are victimized (344c). Thus, according to him, to be unjust is more to one's private advantage than to be just; and the most unjust (the tyrant) is the happiest, whereas the most just is the most wretched (334a). Socrates attacks this argument from a number of angles, but at the end of Book I neither he nor Thrasymachus are convinced it has been refuted, for different reasons.

Thrasymachus seems to present an easy target, in both the form and substance of his comments. His style is abrasive, his tone is arrogant, his goal is victory—preferably unconditional surrender of the humbled opponent. Yet, surprisingly, his may be the voice in Book I that comes closest to speaking for the truly less powerful. It is interesting that he is drawn so negatively by Plato and that commentators see him as adopting "the accents of moral indignation in the cause of immorality."[25]

A. Evidence

If women were present, they would not have needed Glaucon and Adeimantus in Book II to make Thrasymachus' heated claims more understandable. Women would have a plethora of evidence for Socrates to consider regarding the claim that rulers make laws for their own advantage and then declare them to be just for their subjects (338e). In fact, instead of finding evidence only in the standard examples of tyrannies, democracies, and aristocracies (338d), women could introduce for illumination another sort of rule: the rule of men. In a patriarchy, laws are made by men to the advantage of men, but women are called just and good for obeying them despite the fact that it is to their disadvantage. Greek women might have given Socrates examples from then-current marital and property laws of how partial interests masquerade as the common good, as objective justice, perhaps giving rise to a different kind of political analysis. Theorizing about political life with little reference to women or "private" relationships as sources of information or challenges continues today to be a widely accepted practice.

B. Thrasymachus' Truth

The extent to which Socrates finds Thrasymachus to be descriptively correct is murky in the dialogue, since he turns right away to arguments made to prove that true rulers provide for those who are ruled. It seems plausible that Socrates accepts the view that all existing regimes are as Thrasymachus says they are. But this silent assent is a problem, for the lack of attention to the forms and manifestations of unjust rule, as seen by those who are ruled, could lead to incomplete understanding and thus inadequate remedies. Why think imperfect analogies teach more than perfectly representative lived experiences? And, if an earnest communal search for truth is truly Socrates' goal, why does he not know the value of telling his companion where he fully agrees with him? Is such admission unmanly?

Having been on the receiving end of political injustice, perhaps women participants would have raised the question of whether what the rulers consider benefits—money, power, honor—are really to be desired. Freeborn and enslaved women, rich and poor, knew the costs of men's devotion to such supposed goods, knew the harm to others one does by trying to attain them. Perhaps, too, they would challenge Socrates' claim that it is always better to suffer injustice than to be unjust. Confronted with four uneducated women—one sold to a husband, another sold to a brothel, a third beat by a husband who has relations with others too numerous to count, and a fourth confined to her house, not allowed out unescorted—Socrates would find that his assessment of their condition as compared with their violators' would either more truly defend or undermine his position. And how might they have challenged Socrates' notion of a true ruler? Looking not only to their city but also to their households, they might question even the ideal as a figment of an imagination shaped by cultural hierarchy and division.

Conclusion

For many of us at least, the classics can no longer be read as we were taught to read them. [Further,] the standard commentaries . . . [do not] show any awareness of the way in which classic theories are bound up with a defence of masculinity against the dangers of femininity.[26]

One weakness of the Socratic method of question and answer is that questions not raised by a particular set of participants do not get answered, do not even enter into the discussion. It may be true that the absence of female participants in the Platonic dialogues reflects ancient Athenian mores, as the opening quote states. But this essay has argued that it does more than that. It helps to perpetuate those mores.

The conversation in Book I of the *Republic* takes the particular turns it does in great part because of who the participants are. What Book I tells us is how these men experience growing old, what money means to them, what pleasures, fears and hopes they have, and what relations with each other and the gods they see as just. Aging, personal economics, and justice are not, of course, exclusively "male" issues. But when they are discussed in a way that omits mention of women's experiences, relationships, concerns, values, and questions, we are left with what Plato should call "mere opinion," and there is no indication that the parties to the *Republic*'s conversation "know that they do not know."

One needn't subscribe to the existence of *the* Platonic truth to be troubled not only by the barriers to knowledge erected by sexism but by the practical implications of such limited perspectives. The more radical a system of "sex roles," the greater are differences between women's and men's experiences, and the greater are sex differences. Consequently, the more radical the system of sexual differentiation, the greater the dangers are of not having gender-inclusive knowledge. When we understand only what men think and feel of aging, for example, our social policy priorities, medical research agendas, and cultural lore are tainted, at best serving and representing a part of the whole, at worst ignoring, injuring, and invalidating the rest.

To the extent that "all philosophy is a footnote on Plato,"[27] all philosophy is a male patriarchal conversation, in both the questions that have been blessed with the stamp of importance and the viewpoints considered worthy opponents. This affects not only, and perhaps not even most directly, Plato's explicit position on sexual equality. If Plato has raised (though not definitively answered) the major issues that continue to occupy political philosophers, then issues of concern to women in general and to feminists in particular have been, and continue to be, deemed peripheral or irrelevant. In discussions of the "perennial" issues in politics and philosophy, women's different experiences have not been allowed to direct or even enlighten. In this sense the so-called dialogues have silenced more than half the potential speakers, making them male monologues. Contrary to our stereotypes of such things, it is men who do the talking and who, as studies continue to show is the case, decide what gets heard.[28]

The information left out of philosophical dialogue has compromised our understanding of various human conditions. It has, by omission, privileged the perspective of a part of humanity and called that perspective universal and timeless. Those of a different sex, class, and/or race are often left alienated from whatever fruit this philosophy has borne.

When stories either of men or told from a male perspective dominate our theories, women will think theory is not for them or of them. Yet women, rather than philosophy or philosophers, have been seen as the problem. For some time the fact that women were said to be less "turned on" by visual pornography than were men was taken as evidence of women's relatively less sexual nature. But pornography was/is virulently antiwoman, so that women's lack of arousal by it can be seen simply as evidence of women's healthy self-love and empathy for others. That women have also been less "turned on" by traditional philosophy than have men has been used as evidence of women's relative intellectual incapacity. But this philosophy was/is virulently antiwoman, so that women's lack of arousal by it can be seen as evidence of women's strong sense of self and identification with others.

Implicit in this essay is an argument for enlarging the debate over Plato's/Socrates' feminism, for refusing to allow feminism to be reduced to the ancient Athenian equivalent of the twentieth-century practice of measuring feminism by the number of women who are heads of corporations or the number of states with equal rights legislation. Feminism critiques more than corporation leaders, challenging corporate structures, procedures, policies, and profits through its powerful analysis of oppression and violation, on the one hand, and inclusion and empowerment, on the other. Similarly, antifeminism taints more than equal opportunity legislation, influencing, for example, our listing of social priorities and our view of politics as the arena in which the partial interests of self-concerned individuals forever clash. Whatever is said in the *Republic* about women's "official" opportunities or "nature," one cannot conclude from them alone, either way, about the feminism of the text. One example of what is left out of such a reckoning is the bias in selecting which questions to stamp with a seal of significance and which viewpoints to deem worth consideration.

The effects of women's exclusion are substantial. Feminism is about something much more profound than having women say and do what men have said and done, in philosophical dialogue or anywhere else. The philosophical agenda is biased and in need of revisioning. Certain problems and perspectives have been systematically degraded. One of the many paths we need to travel to amend this is the sort of analysis attempted here, an attempt to bring to light, to consciousness, the nearly invisible but ubiquitous bias of a philosophical text.

This essay, of course, has focused only on Book I. I hope this in and of itself is a useful contribution to understanding that text. Certainly commentators almost unanimously treat Book I as centrally important to the *Republic*. But, more strongly, I think it could be argued that the other books, too, marginalize the experiences of all but a minority of men or deal with women only from a male perspective. Book I in this sense is representative of the whole. This is not to say that nothing is left of the dialogue but a presentation of injustice or that parts of it cannot be useful to and even illuminating for feminists as well as others. But elements and influences of bias appear throughout the *Republic*, bias with which we must decide how to contend.

Athens of the fifth century B.C.E. is often portrayed as a somewhat peculiar composition of high culture and slavery, pure democracy for the few and lack of political rights for the rest. Feminist scholarship and activism teach us to doubt the ability to contain or compartmentalize such components. Athenian disdain for women has spillover effects, including effects on the philosophies with which it coexisted. It is insufficient to claim merely that "woman's status in the years of republican Athens was a reproach to the advanced culture and love of the good and the beautiful of which the city of the violet crown was the exponent."[29] Woman's subordinant status was more than a reproach. It was an obstacle, something that compromised the culture as a whole, that affected, for the worse, notions and practices of the good, the beautiful, and the just.

> If philosophy particularly consists in questioning what happens in towns, houses and people's daily lives (and, according to Cicero, such is philosophy's task as seen by Socrates), then the issue of women's lives is necessarily on the agenda. But has it really been so, as an issue in the twenty-five centuries of philosophy that we can observe? Too little or not in the right way, the feminist would say: so here we have an enquiry and a process to be taken further.[30]

Notes

1. Susan Moller Okin, *Women in Western Political Thought* (Princeton, N.J.: Princeton University Press, 1979), 22. Those unfamiliar with Okin's analysis should not read this quote as part of a defense of Plato as a feminist, for that is not her position.

2. Education appears to have been highly differentiated by class and sex. Females were generally educated in the home and for the home. The

poorer were taught housekeeping, and the richer would also learn to spin, weave, and sew. The sons of the wealthy went to school at the earliest age and for the longest time, whereas the sons of the poor started later and ended their public education earlier. Sex segregation was the norm at all ages, as far as I can tell, though it may have been most complete for the sons of the wealthy. As regards age of marriage, a male "frequently . . . waited until he was thirty or over. . . . [G]irls were sometimes married at fifteen, or younger." Charles Gulick, *The Life of the Ancient Greeks* (New York: Cooper Square, 1973; originally published 1902), 119, 122.

3. "Women who survived the exhausting labour of giving birth, as many as ten or twelve times, were probably so worn out by the experience that they could not expect to live beyond the age of thirty-five; many died much earlier. Men could expect to live longer than women by as much as ten years or more." Michael Massey, *Women in Ancient Greece and Rome* (Cambridge: Cambridge University Press, 1988), 6.

4. The social position of women in the "Heroic age" may have been somewhat better. Carroll ascribes the downward shift to the emergence of the city-state and its highly exclusionary practice of citizenship, which entailed surveillance of women for the sake of "legitimate" offspring. I think the relationship was likely more dialectical than that. Mitchell Carroll, *Woman: In All Ages and in All Countries*, vol. 1: *Greek Women* (Philadelphia: Barrie, 1907), 161.

5. In the *Symposium* the priestess Diotima is supposed to be the source of part of the dialogue, but even she does not participate in person.

6. The list of writings dealing with these themes is lengthy. It would include Christine Allen, "Plato on Women," *Feminist Studies* 2 (1975):131–8; Julia Annas, "Plato's *Republic* and Feminism," *Philosophy* 51 (1976): 307–21; Natalie Bluestone, *Women and the Ideal Society: Plato's Republic and Modern Myths of Gender* (Amherst: University of Massachusetts Press, 1987); Anne Dickason, "Anatomy and Destiny: The Role of Biology in Plato's Views of Women," *The Philosophical Forum* 5 (Fall–Winter 1973–1974): 45–53; Lynda Lange, "The Function of Equal Education in Plato's *Republic* and *Laws*," in *The Sexism of Social and Political Theory*, ed. Lorenne Clark and L. Lange (Toronto: University of Toronto Press, 1979): 3–15; H. Lesser, "Plato's Feminism," *Philosophy* 54 (1979): 113–117; Susan Moller Okin, "Philosopher Queens and Private Wives: Plato on Women and the Family," *Philosophy and Public Affairs* 6 (Summer 1977): 345–69; Martha Lee Osborne, "Plato's Unchanging View of Woman: A Denial That Anatomy Spells Destiny," *Philosophical Forum* 6 (Summer 1975): 447–52; Christine Pierce, "Equality: *Republic* V," *The Monist* 57 (January 1973): 1–11; Sarah Pomeroy, "Feminism in Book V of Plato's *Republic*," *Apeiron* 8 (1974): 33–35; Arlene Saxenhouse, "The Philosopher and the Female in the Political Thought of Plato," *Political Theory* 4 (May 1976); Janet Farrell Smith,

"Plato, Irony and Equality," *Women's Studies International Forum* 6 (1983): 597–608; Helen Pringle, "Women in Political Thought," *Hypatia* 8 (Summer 1993): 136–59, and *Engendering Origins*, ed. Bat-Ami Bar-On (Albany: SUNY Press, 1994).

7. Difficulties always arise in talking about Platonic dialogues. Should one treat their content as the views of the speakers in them? As the views of Plato? As opinions representative of the time they were written? Then there are problems specific to Book I of the *Republic*. It is often spoken of as a "Socratic" text rather than a "Platonic" one, and it is thought to have been written at a different time than the rest of the text. My focus here is on the interchanges in Book I, and my stance is to look at them as the words of identifiable speakers also chosen for inclusion in the dialogue by Plato for his own strategic reasons. That is, I think the exchanges say something about the particular participants, about Athenian life, about the *Republic*, and about Plato, and all of these have relevance for a feminist reading of the text.

8. There are, of course, many ways to define a feminist perspective. The insight of radical feminism, that women's own voices must be heard and heeded in doing theory, seems to offer the most fundamental challenge to the patriarchal view that men's traditional experiences have some sort of monopoly on or inherent superiority with respect to virtue, rationality, and/or contribution to the community.

9. Nicholas White writes, "In a preliminary way [Book I] sets up the main issues to be discussed." To the extent this is true, the masculine bias of Book I then has effects on the rest of the text not considered here. *A Companion to Plato's Republic* (Indianapolis: Hackett, 1979), 61.

10. Massey, *Women in Ancient Greece and Rome*, 1.

11. Ibid.

12. References are to Allan Bloom's translation of the *Republic* (New York: Basic Books, 1968). Although Grube's translation (Indianapolis: Hackett, 1974) seems preferable on a number of grounds, I am using Bloom's for two reasons. First, among political scientists it is a popular choice, and I am anxious to confront its presentation of Plato. Second, the translation is accompanied by a 130-page "Interpretive Essay" by Bloom. I would like my reading of his translation to stand in contrast to his, which I consider almost unbelievably blind to issues of gender, race, and class.

13. The Thesmophoria seems to have been one festival "in which women were allowed out of the house, and sexual relations were upset." Ruth Padel, *Women: Model for Possession by Greek Daemons*. Especially see p. 8 for an interesting interpretation.

14. Ernest Barker, *Greek Political Theory* (London: Methuen, 1918), 253.

15. W. K. Lacey, *The Family in Classical Greece* (Ithaca, N.Y.: Cornell University Press, 1968), 159.

16. Alvin Gouldner, *Enter Plato: Classical Greece and the Origins of Social Theory* (New York: Basic Books, 1965), 61. For more on the contest system, also see Nancy Hartsock, *Money Sex and Power: Toward a Feminist Historical Materialism* (Boston: Northeastern University Press, 1983), chap. 8.

17. I take the points in this paragraph from a talk at Purdue University given by Eve Browning Cole, "Women, Slaves, and 'Love of Toil' in Greek Moral Philosophy."

18. Charles Gulick, *The Life of the Ancient Greeks*, 79–81, 124–5.

19. Bloom almost but not quite notes this. "*Apparently* he [Socrates] does not wish to do so [remain with the others]; other activities *might* be more to his taste, and he would like to hurry to them" (310, emphasis added). Yet Bloom, like Polemarchus and friends, needs to assume a conflict of interest to make his next move. For Bloom, Socrates' "apparent" interest in hurrying off elsewhere soon becomes the interest of the philosopher versus the interest of the powerful, obviously and permanently put at odds.

20. Charlotte Perkins Gilman, *Women and Economics: A Study in the Economic Relation between Men and Women as a Factor in Social Evolution* (New York: Harper & Row, 1966; originally published 1898), 333–4.

21. Diana Coole, *Women in Political Theory* (Brighton, Sussex: Wheatsheaf, 1988), 25, emphasis added. Similarly, G. E. M. de Ste. Croix writes, "An Athenian woman could not inherit in her own right, from her father at least: if he died without leaving a natural or adopted son, she as *epikleros* was expected to marry the nearest male relative (who would divorce any wife he might have already), and the property would pass to their male children, thus remaining in the family." *The Class Struggle in the Ancient Greek World* (Ithaca, N.Y.: Cornell University Press, 1981), 101.

22. It is not surprising that the analogies used here and elsewhere generally refer to what men do. The sexes were so segregated in Athens that men probably had little acquaintance with what women did. Still, neither this explanation nor the occasional uses of female analogies (the midwife) mitigate the overall effect.

23. Texts analyzing the connections between patriarchy and violence include Susan Griffin, *Pornography and Silence* (New York: Harper & Row, 1981); Andrea Dworkin, *Woman Hating* (New York: Dutton, 1974); Susan Brownmiller, *Against Our Will* (New York: Bantam Books, 1975); Mary Daly, *Gyn/Ecology* (Boston: Beacon, 1978); Kathleen Barry, *Female Sexual Slavery* (Upper Saddle River, N.J.: Prentice Hall); Adrienne Rich, "Compulsory Heterosexuality and Lesbian Existence," *Signs* 5 (1980); Carole Sheffield, "Sexual Terrorism," in *Women: A Feminist Perspective*, 3rd ed., ed. Jo Freeman (Palo Alto, California: Mayfield, 1984), 3–19; and *Reweaving the Web: Feminism and Nonviolence*, ed. Pam McAllister (Philadelphia: New Society, 1982).

24. Gilman, *His Religion and Hers: A Study of the Faith of Our Fathers and the Work of Our Mothers* (Westport, Conn.: Hyperion, 1976), 95–96.

25. Bloom, *The Republic*, 326.

26. Carole Pateman, "Introduction: The Theoretical Subversiveness of Feminism," in *Feminist Challenges: Social and Political Theory*, ed. Carole Pateman and Elizabeth Gross (Boston: Northeastern University Press, 1986), 2.

27. Whitehead, *Process and Reality* (New York: Macmillan, 1929), 63.

28. Barbara Ehrenreich, "The Politics of Talking in Couples: Conversus Interruptus and Other Disorders," *Ms. Magazine* (May 1981); Deborah Tannen, *You Just Don't Understand: Women and Men in Conversation* (New York: Ballantine, 1990).

29. Carroll, *Woman*, 159–160.

30. Michele Le Doeuff, *Hipparchia's Choice: An Essay Concerning Women, Philosophy, etc.* (Oxford: Blackwell, 1990).

Jean-Jacques Rousseau and Mary Wollstonecraft

I wanted to write this dialogue for a long time before Virginia Sapiro and I had the opportunity to collaborate on it. It is clear that political theory has excluded extraordinarily insightful theorists from its canon because they were female and/or feminist. Women have been contributors to political debates in a number of ways, even though so many act as if the only tradition is that of men writing in response to the writings and actions of other men. Yet just as one should read Rousseau in order to reach the clearest understanding of Wollstonecraft, so one should read Wollstonecraft in order to understand Rousseau more fully.

I loved putting Rousseau and Wollstonecraft side-by-side. I also greatly enjoyed the conversations with Gina as we constructed this. Here they are, together at last!

> The more I worked with Wollstonecraft's texts and with works about her, the more I sensed a violence that has been done not just to her but to many others as well. . . . [W]riting is an act of speech, and participation in political argument is a political activity, especially for those involved in oppositional politics. Wollstonecraft made many dangerous choices as personal and political acts; among them was writing the texts she has left us.
>
> Virginia Sapiro, *A Vindication of Political Virtue*

5

❦ ❦ ❦

Jean-Jacques Rousseau and Mary Wollstonecraft: A(live) Conversation

(This conversation was constructed almost entirely from the writings of Rousseau and Wollstonecraft. Quotation marks indicate what is original. We strove to preserve the sense of the two writers as we understand them; we did not select apparently appropriate quotations out of the context in which they are originally found. Throughout much of this conversation we selected passages where we have reason to believe that Wollstonecraft was indeed responding at least in part to her reading of Rousseau.)

Introductory Thoughts

Our speakers reflect on JJR's work.

JJR: "Childhood is unknown. Starting from the false idea one has of it, the farther one goes, the more one loses one's way" (*Em.* 33). "[I]t would assuredly be the most unbelievable thing in the world that . . . the *Emile* were the work of a man who did not love children" (*Rev.* 125).

MW: March, 1787. Dear Everina, "I am now reading Rousseau's *Emile*, and love his paradoxes. He chuses a *common* capacity to educate—and gives

79

as a reason, that a genius will educate itself—however he rambles into that chimerical world in which I have too often wandered—and draws the usual conclusion that all is vanity and vexation of spirit. He was a strange inconsistent unhappy clever creature—yet he possessed an uncommon portion of sensibility and penetration" (Corr. 1787).

JJR: "I want to inquire whether there can be a legitimate and reliable rule of administration in the civil order, taking men as they are and laws as they can be. I shall try always to reconcile . . . what right permits with what interest prescribes, so that justice and utility are not at variance" (*SC* 46).

MW: "The *Social Contract* of Rousseau, and his admirable work on the origin of the inequalities amongst mankind, had been in the hands of all France, and admired by many, who could not enter into the depth of the reasoning. In short, they were learned by heart, by those whose heads could not comprehend the chain of argument, though they were sufficiently clear to seize the prominent ideas, and act up to their conviction" (*Fr Rev* 61).

JJR: "I have resolved on an enterprise which has no precedent, and which, once complete, will have no imitator. My purpose is to display to my kind a portrait in every way true to nature, and the man I shall portray will be myself. Simply myself. I know my own heart and understand my fellow man" (*Conf.* 17). "I wrote my first *Confessions* . . . in constant anxiety about ways to keep them from the rapacious hands of my persecutors in order to transmit them, if it were possible, to other generations" (*Rev.* 7).

MW: "The *Confessions* . . . will ever be read with interest by those persons of sensibility who have pondered over the movements of their own hearts. . . . [T]hough we must allow that he had many faults which called for the forbearance of his friends, still what have his defects of temper to do with his writings? It is impossible to pursue his simple descriptions without loving the man in spite of the weaknesses of character that he himself depicts, which never appear to have risen from depravity of heart" (Reviews, December 1791).

JJR: "I am now alone on earth . . . I would have loved men in spite of themselves. Only by ceasing to be humane, have they been able to slip away from my affection. . . . But I, detached from them and from everything, what am I? That is what remains for me to seek" (*Rev. 1*).

MW: Dear William, "I am not well—I am hurt—But I mean not to hurt you. Consider what has past as a fever of your imagination; one of the slight mortal shakes to which you are liable—and I—will become again a Solitary Walker" (Corr. 1796).

A first skirmish.

JJR: "By the very law of nature women are at the mercy of men's judgment, as much for their own sake as for that of their children" (*Em.* 364).

MW: "What nonsense! when will a great man arise with sufficient strength of mind to puff away the fumes which pride and sensuality have thus spread over the subject" (*RW* 94).

Both discuss the purpose and reception of their work.

JJR: "I foresee that I will not easily be forgiven for the side I have dared to take. Running counter to everything that men admire today, I can expect only universal blame; and the fact of having been honored by the approval of a few wise men does not allow me to count on the approval of the public. . . . [Fortunately?] I do not care to please either the witty or the fashionable" (*FD* 33).

MW: "My opinion . . . respecting the rights and duties of woman, seems to flow so naturally from the . . . simple principles [that give substance to morality], that I think it scarcely possible, but that some of the enlarged minds who form . . . your admirable constitution, will coincide with me" (*RW* 65).

JJR: "How can one dare blame the sciences before . . . [this] most learned societ[y], praise ignorance in a famous Academy, and reconcile contempt for study with respect for the truly learned? . . . I am not abusing science, I [tell] myself; I am defending virtue before virtuous men" (*FD* 34).

MW: "[M]y arguments . . . are dictated by a disinterested spirit—I plead for my sex—not for myself. . . . It is . . . an affection for the whole human race that makes my pen dart rapidly along to support what I believe to be the cause of virtue" (*RW* 65).

JJR: "[T]he position most advantageous for one with a just cause is to have to defend himself against an upright and enlightened opponent who is judge in his own case" (*FD* 34).

MW: Well, "I aim at being useful!" (*RW* 75).

On Reason

Both floridly celebrate reason.

JJR: "It is a grand and beautiful sight to see man emerge from obscurity somehow by his own efforts; dissipate, by the light of his darkness in which nature had enveloped him; rise above himself; soar intellectually into celestial regions; traverse with giant steps, like the sun, the vastness of the universe; and what is even grander and more difficult come back to himself to study man and know his nature, his duties, and his end" (*FD* 35).

MW: "The utility of collecting a number of facts, and prying into the properties of matter, cannot be contested. To see harmony which subsists in the revolution of the heavenly bodies simply stated, and silently to mark how light and darkness, subsiding as we proceed, enables us to view the fair form of things, calms the mind by cultivating latent seeds of order and taste. We trace in this manner, the footsteps of the Creator, and a kind of elevated humility draws us to the pure source of goodness and perfection for all knowledge rises into importance, as it unites itself to morality" (Reviews, August 1789).

JJR qualifies his celebration: MW does not.

JJR: "If a few men must be allowed to devote themselves to the study of the sciences and arts, it must be only those who feel the strength to walk alone in their footsteps. . . . It is for these few to raise monuments to the glory of human intellect" (*FD* 63).

MW: "*Every* attempt . . . to investigate the human mind, in order to regulate its complicated movements, deserves praise; and the experience of a sagacious individual, will ever throw new light on a subject, intimately connected with the happiness of mankind and the progress of moral improvement" (Reviews, August 1789, our emphasis).

JJR seems to turn on reason altogether.

JJR: On the contrary. "[O]ur souls have been corrupted in proportion to the advancement of our sciences and arts toward perfection. Can it be said that this is a misfortune particular to our age? No, gentlemen; the evils caused by our vain curiosity are as old as the world. The daily ebb and flow of the ocean's waters have not been more steadily subject to the course of the star which gives us light during the night than has the fate of morals and integrity been subject to the advancement of the sciences and arts. Virtue has fled as their light dawned on our horizon, and the same phenomenon has been observed in all times and in all places" (*FD* 39–40).

MW tries to establish common ground.

MW: "In what does man's pre-eminence over the brute creation consist? The answer is as clear as that a half is less than the whole; in Reason. . . . [F]rom the exercise of reason, knowledge and virtue naturally flow" (*RW* 81).

Further on the relationship among reason, passion, and instinct, and the need for education.

JJR: "Conscience, conscience! Divine instinct, immortal and celestial voice, certain guide of a being that is ignorant and limited but intelligent and free; infallible judge of good and bad which makes man like unto God. . . . Without [conscience] I sense nothing in me that raises me above the beasts, other than the sad privilege of leading myself astray from error to error with the aid of an understanding without rule and a reason without principle" (*Em.* 290).

MW: "Conscience, or reason, which you will; for in my view of things, they are synonymous terms" (*RM* 11). "Children are born ignorant, consequently innocent; the passions are neither good nor evil . . . till they receive a direction, and either bound over the feeble barrier raised by a faint glimmering of unexercised reason, called conscience, or strengthen her wavering dictates till sound principles are deeply rooted, and able to cope with . . . headstrong passions. . . . What moral purpose can be answered by extolling good dispositions . . . when [they] . . . are described as instincts: for instinct moves in a direct line to its ultimate end, and asks not for guide and support" (*RM* 31).

On human development and reason.

JJR: Yes, "[w]e are born weak, we need strength; we are born totally unprovided, we need aid; we are born stupid, we need judgment. Everything we do not have at our birth and which we need when we are grown is given us by education" (*Em.* 38). And, indeed, "[b]efore the age of reason we do good and bad without knowing it, and there is no morality in our action" (*Em.* 67).

MW: "Children cannot be taught too early to submit to reason, the true definition of that necessity, which Rousseau insisted on . . . ; for to submit to reason is to submit to the nature of things, and to that God, who formed them so, to promote our real interest" (*RW* 227).

JJR: "To reason with children was Locke's great maxim. . . . I see nothing more stupid than these children who have been reasoned with so much. Of all the faculties of man, reason . . . is the one that develops with the most difficulty and latest. And it is this one which they want to use in order to develop the first faculties! The masterpiece of a good education is to make a reasonable man, and they claim they raise a child by reason! . . . If children understood reason, they would not need to be raised" (*Em.* 89).

MW: "Intellectual improvements, like the growth and formation of the body, must be gradual" (*Thoughts* 10).

JJR: "[B]y speaking to them from an early age a language which they do not understand, one accustoms them to show off with words, to control all that is said to them, to believe themselves as wise as their masters, to become disputatious and rebellious" (*Em.* 89). "Treat your pupil according to his age" (*Em.* 91).

MW: "How then are the tender minds of children to be cultivated? . . . Above all, try to teach them to combine their ideas. It is of more use than can be conceived, for a child to learn to compare things that are similar in some respects, and different in others. I wish them to be taught to think—thinking, indeed, is a severe exercise, and exercise of either mind or body will not at first be entered on, but with a view to pleasure. Not that I would have them make long reflections; for when they do not arise from experience, they are mostly absurd" (*Thoughts* 11). Further, "I am indeed persuaded that the heart, as well as the understanding, is opened by cultivation. . . . And, perhaps, in the education of both sexes, the most difficult task is so to adjust instruction as not to narrow the understanding, whilst the heart is warmed by the generous juices of spring, . . . nor to dry up the feelings by employing the mind in investigations remote from life" (*RW* 135).

Setting the terms of debate on reason and gender.

JJR: Oh, "reason . . . [H]ow many questions are raised by this word! Are [for example] women capable of solid reasoning? Is it important that they cultivate it? Will they succeed in cultivating it? Is its cultivation useful for the functions which are imposed on them? Is it compatible with the simplicity that suits them?" (*Em.* 382).

MW: "[T]he inquiry is whether she have reason or not" (*RW* 122). "[E]ither nature has made a great difference between man and man, or . . . the civilization which has hitherto taken place in the world has been very partial" (*RW* 73). "Women are . . . to be considered either as moral beings, or so weak that they must be entirely subjected to the superior faculties of men" (*RW* 9). "[P]rove. . . . to ward off the charge of injustice and inconsistency, that [women] want reason— else this flaw in your [work] . . . will ever shew that man must, in some shape, act like a tyrant, and tyranny, in whatever part of society it rears its brazen front, will ever undermine morality" (*RW* 68).

Abstract and practical reason.

JJR: Well, "[t]he quest for abstract and speculative truths, principles, and axioms in the sciences, for everything that tends to generalize ideas, is not within the competence of woman" (*Em.* 386).

MW: "[T]he power of generalizing ideas, to any great extent, is not very common amongst men or women" (*RW* 123).

JJR: True, "the art of generalizing ideas . . . is one of the most difficult and belated exercises of human understanding." It is not clear that "the average man [will] ever be capable of deriving his rules of conduct from this manner of reasoning" (*GM* 161). Further, "general and abstract ideas are the source of men's greatest errors" (*Em.* 274). "Thank heaven, we are delivered from all that terrifying apparatus of philosophy. We can be men without being scholars" (*Em.* 290).

Disagreement over
the link between
reason and virtue,
not only, but
especially for
women because of
the nature of
everyday duties.

MW: "Reason comes from God, and is given in whole to each individual, so each individual can be perfected" (*RW* 122). "[I]t is a farce to call any being virtuous whose virtues do not result from the exercise of its own reason" (*RW* 21).

JJR: "The use of reason that leads man to the knowledge of his duties is not very complex. The use of reason that leads woman to the knowledge of hers is even simpler" (*Em.* 382).

MW: "[S]urely, Sir, you will not assert, that a duty can be binding which is not founded on reason? . . . [T]he more understanding women acquire, the more they will be attached to their duty—comprehending it" (*RW* 67).

JJR: "[W]ho would want to spend his life in sterile speculations if each of us, consulting only the duties of man and the needs of nature, had time for nothing except his fatherland, the unfortunate, and his friends?" (*FD* 48).

MW: "I do not mean to insinuate that either sex should be so lost in abstract reflections or distant views, as to forget the affections and duties that lie before them. . . . [O]n the contrary, I would warmly recommend them, even while I assert, that they afford most satisfaction when they are considered in their true, sober, light." For example, "[c]onnected with man as daughters, wives, and mothers, [women's] moral character may be estimated by their manner of fulfilling those simple duties; but the end, the grand end of their exertions should be to unfold [their] own faculties and acquire the dignity of conscious virtue" (*RW* 95).

JJR: "A brilliant wife is a plague to her husband, her children, her friends, her valets, everyone.

From the sublime elevation of her fair genius she disdains all her woman's duties" (*Em.* 409). "In general, if it is important for men to limit their studies to useful knowledge, it is even more important for women, because . . . their lives do not permit them to indulge themselves in any preferred talent to the prejudice of their duties" (*Em.* 368).

MW: "I . . . infer that reason is absolutely necessary to enable a woman to perform any duty properly, and I must . . . repeat, that sensibility is not reason" (*RW* 133). "Rousseau was more consistent when he wished to stop the progress of reason in both sexes, for if men eat of the tree of knowledge, women will come in for a taste; but from the imperfect cultivation which their understandings now receive, they only attain a knowledge of evil" (*RW* 89).

JJR sees some exceptions to the rule of ignorance for women.

JJR: "I would not indiscriminately object to a woman's being limited to the labors of her sex alone and left in profound ignorance of all the rest. But . . . such a woman would be too easy to seduce. . . . Moreover, since she is subject to the judgment of men, she ought to merit their esteem. . . . How will she go about all this if she is ignorant of our institutions, if she knows nothing of our practices and our proprieties, if she knows neither the source of human judgments nor the passions determining them?" (*Em.* 382–83). Finally, "how will a woman who has no habit of reflecting raise her children? How will she discern what suits them? How will she incline them toward virtues she does not know, toward merit of which she has no idea?" (*Em.* 408–9).

MW presses the point.

MW: "How indeed [will] she, when her husband is not always at hand to lend her his reason?—

when they both together make but one moral being" (*RW* 89). "[T]his duty [of caring for children] would afford many forcible arguments for strengthening the female understanding, if it were *properly* considered" (*RW* 222, our emphasis). "To be a good mother—a woman must have sense, and that independence of mind which few women possess who are taught to depend entirely on their husbands. . . . [U]nless the understanding of woman be enlarged, and her character rendered more firm, by being allowed to govern her own conduct, she will never have sufficient sense or command of temper to manage her children properly" (*RW* 223).

JJR: Whatever women might be capable of, "[a]ll their studies ought to be related to practice." "[T]he art of thinking is not foreign to women, but they ought only to skim the sciences of reasoning" (*Em.* 426).

MW: "[T]he knowledge of the two sexes should be the same in nature. . . . [W]omen, considered not only as moral, but rational creatures, ought to endeavor to acquire human virtues (or perfections) by the same means as men, instead of being educated like a fanciful kind of half being—one of Rousseau's wild chimeras" (*RW* 108).

JJR: "If woman could ascend to general principles as well as man can, and if man had as good a mind for details as woman does, they would always be independent of one another, they would live in eternal discord, and their partnership could not exist" (*Em.* 377).

MW: "If marriage be the cement of society, mankind should be educated after the same model, or the intercourse of the sexes will never deserve the name of fellowship, nor will women ever fulfill the peculiar duties of their sex, till they become enlightened citizens, till they become free by being enabled to earn their own subsistence, independent of men; in the same manner, I mean, to prevent misconstruction, as one man is independent of another. Nay, marriage will never be held sacred till women, by being brought up with men, are prepared to be their companions rather than their mistresses. . . . So convinced am I of this truth that I will venture to predict that virtue will never prevail in society till the virtues of both sexes are founded on reason; and till the affections common to both are allowed to gain their due strength by the discharge of mutual duties" (*RW* 237).

On Gender

They begin with some basic agreement about natural similarity.

JJR: "In everything not connected with sex, woman is man. She has the same organs, the same needs, the same faculties. The machine is constructed in the same way; its parts are the same; the one functions as does the other; the form is similar; and in whatever respect one considers them, the difference between them is only one of more or less" (*Em.* 357). "Up to the nubile age children of the two sexes have nothing apparent to distinguish them: the same visage, the same figure, the same complexion, the same voice. Everything is equal: girls are children, boys are children; the same name suffices for beings so much alike" (*Em.* 211).

They differ on the education and social construction of women and men.

MW: "A wild wish has just flown from my heart to my head, and I will not stifle it though it may excite a horse-laugh.—I do earnestly wish to see the distinction of sex confounded in society, unless where love animates the behaviour" (*RW* 125).

JJR: On the other hand, "[a] perfect woman and a perfect man ought not to resemble each other in mind any more than in looks" (*Em.* 358).

MW: "I wish to throw down my gauntlet, and deny the existence of sexual virtues, not excepting modesty. For man and woman, truth, if I understand the meaning of the word, must be the same" (*RW* 120).

JJR: "[M]an and woman are not and ought not to be constituted in the same way in either character or temperament[;] it follows that they ought not to have the same education" (*Em.* 363).

MW: "[F]alse system[s] of education . . . consider[. . .] females rather as women than human creatures" (*RW* 73).

JJR: "To cultivate man's qualities in women and to neglect those which are proper to them is obviously to work to their detriment. . . . [T]he two are incompatible" (*Em.* 364).

MW: "[F]rom every quarter have I heard exclamations against masculine women; but where are they to be found? If by this appellation men mean to inveigh against their ardour in hunting, shooting, and gaming, I shall most cordially join in the cry; but if it be against the imitation of manly virtues, or, more properly speaking, the attainment of those talents and virtues, the exercise of which ennobles the human character, and which raise females in the scale of animal being, when they are comprehensively termed mankind;—all those who view them with a philosophic eye must, I should think, wish with me, that they may every day grow more and more masculine" (*RW* 74).

JJR: "[J]udicious mother, do not make a decent man of your daughter" (*Em.* 364).

MW: "The mother, who wishes to give true dignity of character to her daughter" must do the opposite of what Rousseau says "with all the deluding charms of eloquence and philosophical sophistry" (*RW* 110).

Women as subjects of men.

JJR: "In the union of the sexes . . . [o]ne ought to be active and strong, the other passive and weak. One must necessarily will and be able; it suffices that the other put up little resistance. Once this principle is established, it follows that woman is made specially to please man. If man ought to please her in turn, it is due to a less direct necessity. His merit is in his power; he pleases by the sole fact of his strength. . . . If woman is made to please and to be subjugated, she ought to make herself agreeable to man" (*Em.* 356).

MW: "I have quoted this passage, lest my readers should suspect that I warped the author's reasoning to support my own arguments. . . . [I]n educating women [Rousseau's] fundamental principles lead to a system of cunning and lasciviousness. Supposing woman to have been formed only to please, and be subject to man, the conclusion is just, she ought to sacrifice every other consideration to render herself agreeable to him: and let this brutal desire of self-preservation be the grand spring of all her actions, when it is proved to be the iron bed of fate. . . . But . . . I may be allowed to doubt whether woman was created for man" (*RW* 148). Yours and other "books . . .

tend, in my opinion, to degrade one half of the human species, and render women pleasing at the expense of every solid virtue" (*RW* 91).

The dependence of ruler and ruled.

JJR: Well, "[w]oman and man are made for one another, but their mutual dependence is not equal. Men depend on women because of their desires; women depend on men because of both their desires and their needs" (*Em.* 364).

MW: "Whilst man remains such an imperfect being as he appears hitherto to have been, he will . . . be the slave of his appetites; and those women obtaining most power who gratify a predominant one, the sex is degraded by a physical, if not by a moral necessity" (*RW* 116).

JJR: "[W]oman [has] more facility to excite the desires than man to satisfy them. This causes the latter, whether he like it or not, to depend on the former's wish and constraints him to seek to please her in turn" (*Em.* 360). "Is it our fault that they please us when they are pretty, that their mincing ways seduce us, that the art which they learn from you attracts us and pleases us, that we like to see them tastefully dressed, that we let them sharpen at their leisure the weapons with which they subjugate us?" (*Em.* 363).

MW: "My own sex, I hope, will excuse me, if I treat them like rational creatures, instead of flattering their fascinating graces, and viewing them as if they were in a state of perpetual childhood" (*RW* 75). "I lament that women are systematically degraded by receiving the trivial attentions, which men think it manly to pay to the sex, when, in fact, they are insultingly supporting their own superiority" (*RW* 125). "Who ever drew a more exalted female character than Rous-

seau? though in the lump he constantly endeav-
oured to degrade the sex. And why was he thus
anxious? Truly to justify himself the affection
which weakness and virtue had made him cherish for that fool Theresa. He could not raise her
to the common level of her sex; and therefore he
laboured to bring women down to hers" (*RW*
246).

The sexual basis of appropriate gender relations.

JJR: Consider the origin of "attack and defense,
the audacity of one sex and the timidity of the
other. . . . Who could think that nature has indiscriminately prescribed the same advances to both
men and women, and that the first to form desires should also be the first to show them? . . .
Since the undertaking has such different *consequences* for the two sexes, is it natural that they
should have the same audacity in abandoning
themselves to it? With so great an inequality in
what each risks in the union, how can one fail to
see that if reserve did not impose on one sex the
moderation which nature imposes on the other,
the result would soon be the ruin of both, and
then mankind would perish by the means established for preserving it?" (*Em.* 358–59).

MW: "Men are more subject to the physical love
than women. I know of no other way of preserving the chastity of mankind, than that of rendering women rather objects of love than desire. The
difference is great" (*Hints* 272). "The want of
modesty . . . arises from the state of warfare so
strenuously supported by voluptuous men as the
very essence of modesty, though, in fact, its
bane" (*RW* 195). "It is vain to expect much public
or private virtue, till both men and women grow
more modest—till men, curbing a sensual fond-
ness for the sex, or an affectation of manly assur-

ance, more properly speaking, impudence, treat each other with respect" (*RW* 195). "Till men are more chaste, women will be immodest" (*RW* 196).

On appearances
and reputation.

JJR: "Doubtless it is not permitted to anyone to violate his faith, and every unfaithful husband who deprives his wife of the only reward of the austere duties of her sex is an unjust and barbarous man. But the unfaithful woman does more; she dissolves the family and breaks all the bonds of nature. In giving the man children which are not his, she betrays both. She joins perfidy to infidelity. . . . If there is a frightful condition in the world, it is that of an unhappy father who, lacking confidence in his wife, does not dare to yield to the sweetest sentiments of his heart, who wonders, in embracing his child, whether he is embracing another's, the token of his dishonor, the plunderer of his own children's property. . . . It is important, then, not only that a woman be faithful, but that she be judged to be faithful by her husband, by those near her, by everyone. . . . [S]he [should] give evidence of her virtue to the eyes of others as well as to her own conscience" (*Em.* 361). "Opinion is the grave of virtue among men and its throne among women" (*Em.* 365).

MW: "Women are told from their infancy, and taught by the example of their mothers, that a little knowledge of human weakness, justly termed cunning, softness of temper, outward obedience, and a scrupulous attention to a puerile kind of propriety, will obtain for them the protection of man" (*RW* 88); and "should they be beautiful, every thing else is needless, for, at least, twenty years of their lives" (*RW* 88). "Exterior accomplishments are not to be obtained by imitation, they must result from the mind, or the deception is soon detected, and admiration gives place to contempt" (*Reader* 59). Besides, "faithless husbands will make faithless wives" (*RW* 68).

JJR: "From . . . habitual constraint comes a docility which women need all their lives, since they never cease to be subjected either to a man or to the judgments of men and they are never permitted to put themselves above these judgments" (*Em.* 370).

MW: "Who made man the exclusive judge, if woman partake with him the gift of reason?" (*RW* 67).

JJR: "The first and most important quality of a woman is gentleness. As she is made to obey a being who is so imperfect, often so full of vices, and always so full of defects as man, she ought to learn early to endure even injustice and to bear a husband's wrongs without complaining. It is not for his sake, it is for her own, that she ought to be gentle. The bitterness and the stubbornness of women never do anything but increase their ills and the bad behaviour of their husbands" (*Em.* 370).

MW: "Formed to live with such an imperfect being as man, they ought to learn from the exercise of their faculties the necessity of forbearance; but all the sacred rights of humanity are violated by insisting on blind obedience; or, the most sacred rights belong only to man. The being who patiently endures injustice, and silently bears insults, will soon become unjust, or unable to discern right from wrong. . . . Of what materials can that heart be composed, which can melt when insulted, and instead of revolting at injustice, kiss

the rod? . . . Nature never dictated such insincer-
ity. . . . Let the husband beware of trusting too
implicitly to this servile obedience; for if his wife
can with winning sweetness caress him when
angry, and when she ought to be angry, unless
contempt has stifled a natural effervescence, she
may do the same after parting with a lover" (*RW*
153).

More on the
dependencies of the
masters and the
powers of the weak.

JJR: In fact, "the stronger appears to be master
but actually depends on the weaker. This is due
not to a frivolous practice of gallantry or to the
proud generosity of a protector, but to an invari-
able law of nature which gives woman more facility to excite the desires than man to satisfy them.
This causes the latter, whether he likes it or not,
to depend on the former's wish and constrains
him to seek to please her in turn, so that she will
consent to let him be the stronger" (*Em.* 360).

MW: "Women, . . . obtaining power by unjust
means, . . . become either abject slaves or capri-
cious tyrants" (*RW* 114). "When men boast of
their triumphs over women, what do they boast
of?" (*RW* 195).

JJR: "[W]hat is sweetest for man in his victory is
the doubt whether it is weakness which yields to
strength or the will which surrenders. And the
woman's usual ruse is always to leave this doubt
between her and him" (*Em.* 360).

MW: "I . . . exclaim against the sexual desire of
conquest when the heart is out of the question"
(*RW* 125). "How grossly do they insult us who
thus advise us only to render ourselves gentle,
domestic brutes! For instance, the winning softness so warmly, and frequently, recommended,
that governs by obeying. What childish expres-

sions, and how insignificant is the being . . . who will condescend to govern by such sinister methods!" (*RW* 89).

On the value of weakness.

JJR: "Far from blushing at their weakness, [women] make it their glory. Their tender muscles are without resistance. They pretend to be unable to lift the lightest burdens. They would be ashamed to be strong. Why is that? It is not only to appear delicate; it is due to a shrewder precaution. They prepare in advance excuses and the right to be weak in case of need" (*Em.* 360).

MW: "Rousseau has furnished [women] with a plausible excuse . . . to be proud of a defect, which could only have occurred to a man, . . . that they might, forsooth, have a pretext for yielding to a natural appetite without violating a romantic species of modesty, which gratifies the pride and libertinism of man" (*RW* 109). "[T]his artificial weakness produces a propensity to tyrannize, and gives birth to cunning, the natural opponent of strength, which leads [women] to play off those contemptible infantine airs that undermine esteem even whilst they excite desire" (*RW* 77).

JJR: "[Men] constantly say, 'Women have this or that failing which we do not have.' [Their] pride deceives [them]. They would be failings for [men]; they are [women's] good qualities" (*Em.* 363).

MW: "As a philosopher, I read with indignation the plausible epithets which men use to soften their insults; and, as a moralist, I ask what is meant by such heterogeneous association, as fair defects, amiable weaknesses, &c?" (*RW* 103).

JJR: "The peculiar cleverness given to the fair sex is a very equitable compensation for their lesser share of strength, a compensation without which women would be not man's companion but his slave. It is by means of this superiority in talent that she keeps herself his equal and that she governs him while obeying him. Woman has everything against her—our defects, her timidity, and her weakness. She has in her favor only her art and her beauty. Is it not just that she cultivate both?" (*Em.* 371).

MW: "[T]he arbitrary power of beauty . . ." (*RW* 90). "Let me reason with the supporters of this opinion who have any knowledge of human nature, do they imagine that marriage can eradicate the habitude of life? The woman who has only been taught to please will soon find that her charms are oblique sunbeams, and that they cannot have much effect on her husband's heart when they are seen every day, when summer is passed and gone" (*RW* 96). "[T]he great art of pleasing . . . is only useful to a mistress; the chaste wife, and serious mother, should only consider her power to please as the polish of her virtues. . . . [H]er first wish should be to make herself respectable" (*RW* 97).

JJR: "[T]here is quite a difference between wanting to please the man of merit, the truly lovable man, and wanting to pleasure those little flatterers who dishonor both their own sex and the one they imitate" (*Em.* 365).

The need for independence.

MW: "To gain the affections of a virtuous man is affectation necessary?" (*RW* 97). "Besides, the woman who strengthens her body and exercises her mind will . . . *merit* his regard, she will not find it necessary to conceal her affection, nor to pretend to an unnatural coldness of constitution to excite her husband's passions" (*RW* 987, our emphasis). "Men have superior strength of body; but were it not for mistaken notions of beauty, women would acquire sufficient to enable them to earn their own subsistence, the true definition of independence" (*RW* 155).

Duty and
occupation.

JJR: "Is it not a sound way of reasoning to present exceptions in response to such well-grounded general laws? Women, you say, do not always produce children? No, but their proper purpose is to produce them. . . . Finally, what does it matter that this or that woman produces few children? Is woman's status any less that of motherhood, and is it not by general laws that nature and morals ought to provide for this status? Even if there were intervals as long as one supposes between pregnancies, will a woman abruptly and regularly change her way of life without peril and risk? Will she be nurse today and warrior tomorrow? . . . Will she suddenly go from shade, enclosure, and domestic cares to the harshness of the open air, the labors, the fatigues, and the perils of war?" (*Em* 262).

MW: "As a proof of the inferiority of the sex, Rousseau has . . . exclaimed How can they leave the nursery for the camp! . . . Fair and softly, gentle reader, male or female, do not alarm thyself, for though I have compared the character of a modern soldier with that of a civilized woman, I am not going to advise them to turn their distaff into a musket, though I sincerely wish to see the bayonet converted into a pruning hook. I only recreated an imagination . . . by supposing that society will some time or other be so constituted, that man must necessarily fulfill the duties of a citizen, or be despised, and that while he was employed in any of the departments of civil life, his wife, also an active citizen, should be equally intent to manage her family, educate her children, and assist her neighbors. But, to render her really virtuous and useful, she must not, if she discharge her civil duties, want, individually the protection of civil laws; she must not be dependent on her husband's bounty for her subsistence during his life, or support after his death—for how can a being be generous who has nothing of its own? or virtuous, who is not free?" (*RW* 216–17).

JJR: "If I were sovereign, I would permit sewing and the needle trades only to women and to cripples reduced to occupations like theirs" (*Em.* 199).

MW: "Women might certainly study the art of healing, and be physicians as well as nurses. And midwifery, decency seems to allot to them" (*RW* 218). "Business of various kinds, they might likewise pursue, if they were educated in a more orderly manner, which might save many from common and legal prostitution. Women would not then marry for . . . support" (*RW* 218). "I may excite laughter, by dropping a hint, which I mean to pursue, some future time, for I really think that women ought to have representatives, instead of being arbitrarily governed without having any direct share allowed them in the deliberations of government" (*RW* 217).

On power and inequality.

JJR: "So, decide to raise them like men. . . . The more women want to resemble [men], the less women will govern them, and then men will truly be the masters" (*Em.* 363).

MW: " 'Educate women like men,' says Rousseau, 'and the more they resemble our sex the less power will they have over us.' This is the very point I aim at. I do not wish them to have power over men; but over themselves" (*RW* 131).

JJR: "When woman complains . . . about unjust manmade inequality, she is wrong. This inequality is not a human institution—or, at least, it is the work not of prejudice but of reason" (*Em.* 361).

MW: "Surely it is *madness* to make the fate of thousands depend on the caprice of a weak fellow creature, whose very station sinks him necessarily below the meanest of his subjects!" (*RW* 85, our emphasis).

JJR: "[I]n relations between men, the worst that can happen to someone *is* for him to see himself at the discretion of someone else" (*SD* 72, our emphasis).

MW: "[A]ll power inebriates weak man; and its abuse proves that the more equality there is established among men, the more virtue and happiness will reign in society" (*RW* 85).

JJR: "One who believes himself the master of others is nonetheless a greater slave than they" (*SC* 46).

MW: "Let there be then no coercion *established* in society" (*RW* 68).

JJR: "Force is a physical power. I do not see what morality can result from its effects" (*SC* 48).

MW: "Do you not act a similar part, when you *force* all women, by denying them civil and political rights, to remain immured in their families groping in the dark?" (*RW* 67).

On Inequality

A more general discussion on inequality ensues, with much agreement.

JJR: "[D]isastrous inequality [is] introduced among men by the distinction of talents and the debasement of virtues. . . . One no longer asks if a man is upright, but rather if he is talented; nor of a book if it is useful, but if it is well written. Rewards are showered on the witty, and virtue is left without honors" (*FD* 58).

On class and property.

MW: "One class presses on another; for all are aiming to procure respect on account of their property: and property, once gained, will procure the respect due only to talents and virtue. Men neglect the duties incumbent on man, yet are treated like demigods; . . . There must be more equality established in society, or morality will never gain ground" (*RW* 211).

JJR: "The first person who, having fenced off a plot of ground, took it into his head to say *this is mine* and found people simple enough to believe him, was the true founder of civil society. What crimes, wars, murders, what miseries and horrors would the human race have been spared by someone who, uprooting the stakes or filling in the ditch, had shouted to his fellow-men: Beware of listening to this imposter; you are lost if you forget that the fruits belong to all and the earth to no one!" (*SD* 141–42).

MW: "The demon of property has ever been at hand to encroach on the sacred rights of men, and to fence round with awful pomp laws that war with justice" (*RM* 9). "From the respect paid to property flow, as from a poisoned fountain, most of the evils and vices which render this world such a dreary scene" (*RW* 211).

JJR: "It is precisely because the force of things always tends to destroy equality that the force of legislation should always tend to maintain it" (*SC* 75).

MW: Precisely. "Nature having made men unequal, by giving stronger bodily and mental powers to one than to another, the end of government ought to be, to destroy this inequality by protecting the weak. Instead of which, it has always leaned to the opposite side, wearing itself out by disregarding the first principle of its organization" (*Fr Rev* 17).

JJR poses the common analogy of family and state.

JJR: "The family is . . . the prototype of political societies. The leader is like the father, the people are like the children; and since all are born equal and free they only alienate their freedom for their utility" (*SC* 47).

MW once again presses the analogy by arguing for a small republic.

MW: "A man has been termed a microcosm; and every family might also be called a state. States, it is true, have mostly been governed by arts that disgrace the character of man" (*RW* 249). But as for the family, "I exclaim against the laws which throw the whole weight of the yoke on the weaker shoulder, and force women, when they claim protectorship as mothers, to sign a contract, which renders them dependent on the caprice of the tyrant, whom choice or necessity has appointed to reign over them. Various are the cases, in which a woman ought to separate herself from her husband" (*Wrongs* 179).

JJR returns to his main subject.

JJR: Even when "government and laws provide for the safety and well-being of assembled men, the sciences, letters and the arts, less despotic and perhaps more powerful, spread garlands of flowers over the iron chains with which men are burdened, stifle in them the sense of that original liberty for which they seem to have been born, make them love their slavery, and turn them into what is called civilized peoples" (*FD* 36).

MW agrees with his point but turns it to her purpose.

MW: Just like "those pretty feminine phrases, which the men condescendingly use to soften our slavish dependence" (*RW* 75). "Thus degraded, her reason . . . is employed rather to burnish than to snap her chains" (*RW* 171). "Men . . . submit every where to oppression, when they have only to lift up their heads to throw off the yoke." "Women, I argue from analogy, are degraded by the same propensity . . . and, at last, despise the freedom which they have not sufficient virtue to struggle to attain" (*RW* 121). "Equality," you know, "will not rest firmly even when founded on a rock, if one half of mankind be chained to its bottom by fate, for they will be continually undermining it through ignorance or pride" (*RW* 211). "Still harping on the same subject, you will exclaim—How can I avoid it, when most of the struggles of an uneventful life have been occasioned by the oppressed state of my sex; we reason deeply, when we forcibly feel" (Scand. 25).

JJR pursues the subject of the value of passion.

JJR: "Whatever our moralists say, human understanding owes much to the passions. . . . It is by the activity of the passions that our reason improves itself; we seek to know only because we desire to enjoy; and it is impossible to conceive a man who had neither desires nor fears giving himself the trouble of reasoning" (*SD* 189).

MW substantially agrees.

MW: "Poetry certainly flourishes most in the first rude state of society. The passions speak most eloquently, when they are not shackled by reason" (*Hints*). But "for what purpose were the passions implanted? That man by struggling with them might attain a degree of knowledge denied to brutes" (*RW* 81). "Our passions will not contribute much to our bliss, till they are under the dominion of reason, and till that reason is enlightened and improved" (*Thoughts* 37).

JJR parts from her on the blessings of civilization.

JJR: "[I]t must . . . be agreed that the more violent the passions, the more necessary laws are to constrain them. But the disorders and crimes these passions cause every day among us show well enough the inadequacy of laws in this regard, it would still be good to examine whether these disorders did not arise with the laws themselves; for then, even should they be capable of repressing these disorders, the very least that ought to be required of the laws is to stop an evil which would not exist without them" (*SD* 134). "Let us being by distinguishing the moral and the physical in the sentiment of love. The physical is that general desire which inclines one sex to unite with the other. The moral is that which determines this desire and fixes it exclusively on a single object. . . . Now it is easy to see that the moral element of love is an artificial sentiment born of the usage of society and extolled with much skill and care by women in order to establish their ascendancy and make dominant the sex that ought to obey. . . . It is therefore incontestable that love itself, like all the other passions, has acquired only in society that impetuous ardor which so often makes it fatal for men" (*SD* 134–135).

Their differences are maintained.

MW: "Women as well as men ought to have the common appetites and passions of their nature, they are only brutal when unchecked by reason" (*RW* 200). "When we contemplate the infancy of man, his gradual advance toward maturity, his miserable weakness as a solitary being, and the crudeness of his first notions respecting the nature of civil society, it will not appear extraordinary, that the acquirement of political knowledge has been so extremely slow, or that public happiness has not been more rapidly and generally diffused" (*Fr Rev* 15). "Our ancestors have laboured for us; and we, in our turn, must labour for posterity. It is by tracing the mistakes, and profiting from the discoveries of one generation, that the next is able to take a more elevated stand" (*Fr Rev* 183). "Rousseau exerts himself to prove that all was right originally: a crowd of authors that all is now right: and I, that all will be right" (*RW* 84).

Concluding Thoughts

A reminder of MW's respect for JJR.

MW: "He was a strange inconsistent and unhappy clever creature—yet he possessed an uncommon portion of sensibility and penetration" (Scand. 145). He was "an author so thoroughly acquainted with the human heart" (Reviews 49).

And, indeed, her identification with him.

"Rousseau's literary station has long been settled by time on a firm basis; his genius spreads flowers over the most barren tract, yet his profound sagacity and paradoxical caprice; his fascinating eloquence and specious errors, may be seen by their own light" (Reviews 136). "[T]he excess of his affection for his fellow-creatures, his exquisite sensibility, and that panting after distinction, so characteristic of genius, all contributed to render his conduct strange and inexplicable to little minds" (Reviews 231–32).

Afterthoughts

Sapiro

Rousseau, of course, was dead before he could have heard of Wollstonecraft. As I have argued previously (*A Vindication of Political Virtue: The Political Theory of Mary Wollstonecraft* [Chicago: University of Chicago Press, 1992]), Wollstonecraft's intellectual relationship with Rousseau was intriguing. Those who have read only *The Rights of Woman*, especially if they have attended only to the surface arguments about women's education, may imagine she found him wholly lacking in merit. A closer examination of her work leads to a different conclusion. Rousseau served as a leitmotif in Wollstonecraft's life; he reappears regularly in her writing not just as a canonical father but as a representative of certain ideas and struggles in her thinking. Like the later musical technique of the leitmotif, Rousseau sometimes stands in the foreground as the main subject, as in the *Vindication of the Rights of Woman* and some of Wollstonecraft's reviews; sometimes his presence can be discerned as a context or further explanation of the main subject, as in *Mary* and *A Short Residence*, or in her struggles with personal issues and problems, as we see, for example, in her reference to the *Solitary Walker* in her correspondence with William Godwin. She often seems to have returned to Rousseau when she was contemplating a difficult intellectual or emotional problem. She used much the same words to characterize his personal and emotional character as she used to describe her own.

With what works of Rousseau was Wollstonecraft familiar? And how well did she know them? It is important to remember, in her reading of Rousseau, that she was a devotee of his works, but she was not a scholar; many scholars would no doubt quibble with her interpretations of him. Her writings indicate with great certainty that she had read *La Nouvelle Heloise*, *Emile*, *The Confessions*, and *The Reveries of the Solitary Walker*. She probably read *A Discourse on Inequality* and the *Letter to D'Alembert*. She may have read the *Social Contract*, but she may have been familiar with it only through reputation. In her career as a reviewer, she reviewed many works by and about Rousseau, including the second part of *The Confessions* and volumes entitled *Thoughts of Jean-Jacques Rousseau, Citizen of Geneva; The Beauties of Rousseau; Letters on the Works and Character of J. J. Rousseau* by Mme. de Stael; *Laura; or Original Letters;* and *Letters on the Confessions of J. J. Rousseau.*

Weiss

In this essay, as in others collected here, more than one conversation is taking place. The exchanges between Rousseau and Wollstonecraft constitute the most obvious dialogue. The two of them are also present as representatives of a larger conversation, that between mainstream and feminist traditions in political theory. There were many interesting conversations between Gina and myself as we compiled it. Finally, the script is a means for us to convey certain messages.

I had four ideas about Wollstonecraft I wanted to give voice to by assembling this dialogue. First, I wanted to correct the mistaken impression—conveyed in so much of the literature on Wollstonecraft—that Wollstonecraft simply condemned and rejected Rousseau's political analysis. This dialogue contains evidence that she admired Rousseau's work and established a great deal of common ground with him on issues of central importance to both of them. He does not emerge as a prominent figure in her work just as a straw figure, just as evidence of inconsistent, misguided, or misogynist politics. It would hardly have been worth the amount of thoughtful analysis given to Rousseau, and would not have required it, simply to reject him.

Wollstonecraft's subtle appreciation of Rousseau connects to my second message. I believe this dialogue presents some of the evidence for my claim that no one has offered a better critique of Rousseau than Wollstonecraft constructed over two centuries ago. And I believe that part of the reason her critique is so exemplary is that there *is* acknowledged common ground between the two. She offers a devastating internal critique, saying to Rousseau that if indeed we care about such things as active citizenship and virtue, the public and private role of women must be radically altered. She talked to Rousseau in terms he could recognize and respect, neither ignoring nor talking past him. Although he did not have the opportunity to respond to her as she did to him, I would argue, and have argued elsewhere (*Gendered Community: Rousseau, Sex and Politics* [New York: New York University Press, 1993]), that his political analysis is ultimately incapable of satisfactorily answering the political challenges she raises or of refuting her arguments against him.

Again, this point leads to the third message I wanted to send. For contemporary feminist theorists, Wollstonecraft points out, almost as clearly as one could hope for, the precise moments when Rousseau's analysis merges with antifeminist thinking and when it could go otherwise. She does that by showing where it is that she travels with him and where she departs. Wollstonecraft thus addresses a question that continues to attract feminist theorists today: how inextricable a part of his political analysis is Rousseau's antifeminism? As Diana Coole phrases the issue:

> The question remains whether political theorists can continue to read *The Social Contract* as though it were a gender-neutral text and Rousseau's misogyny elsewhere an expendable aberration, or whether in fact the role he gives to women in *Emile* is an essential component of his plan for social regeneration.[1]

Even today we can look for no better answer to this question than that sympathetically and critically drawn by Wollstonecraft.

Finally, I wanted to be able to convey some of what political theory has lost by silencing people like Wollstonecraft. No one in the canon offers the critique of Rousseau she makes. Without her, the historical conversation about Rousseau is misrepresented and incomplete. This final point pertains not only to Wollstonecraft (or to Rousseau) but to the still uncounted, unread, untranslated, unstudied ideas of so many others in the history of political thought and action.

Sources

Work used for citation in this conversation:

Rousseau

Conf.   *The Confessions of Jean-Jacques Rousseau.* Translation and notes by J. M. Cohen. New York: Penguin, 1978.

Em.   *Emile; or, On Education.* Introduction, translation, and notes by Allan Bloom. New York: Basic Books, 1979.

FD   *Discourse on the Sciences and Arts (First Discourse).* In *The First and Second Discourses,* ed. Roger D. Master, trans. Roger D. Masters and Judith R. Masters. New York: St. Martin's, 1964.

GM   *Geneva Manuscript* (first version of *On the Social Contract*). In *On the Social Contract with Geneva Manuscript and Political Economy,* ed. Roger D. Masters, trans. Judith R. Masters. New York: St. Martin's, 1978.

Rev.   *The Reveries of the Solitary Walker.* Translation with preface, notes, and an interpretive essay by Charles E. Butterworth. New York: Harper Colophon Books, 1982.

SC   *On the Social Contract: or, Principles of Political Right.* In *On the Social Contract with Geneva Manuscript and Political Economy,* ed. Roger D. Masters, trans. Judith R. Masters. New York: St. Martin's, 1978.

SD   *Discourse on the Origin and Foundations of Inequality (Second Discourse).* In *The First and Second Discourses,* ed. Roger D. Masters, trans. Roger D. Masters and Judith R. Masters. New York: St. Martin's Press, 1964.

Wollstonecraft

The editions of all of the works except the letters are from Janet Todd and Marilyn Butler, eds., *The Works of Mary Wollstonecraft* (New York: New York University Press, 1989). The correspondence of Wollstonecraft (abbreviated Corr.) are found in Ralph M. Wardle, ed., *Collected Letters of Mary Wollstonecraft* (Ithaca, N.Y.: Cornell University Press, 1979).

Corr.   Correspondence

Fr Rev   *An Historical and Moral View of the Origin and Progress of the French Revolution,* 1794

Reader   *The Female Reader,* 1789

RM   *A Vindication of the Rights of Men,* 1790

RW   *A Vindication of the Rights of Woman,* 1792

Scand.   *Letters Written during a Short Residence in Sweden, Norway, and Denmark,* 1796

Thoughts *Thoughts on the Education of Daughters,* 1788

Wrongs   *The Wrongs of Woman; or, Maria,* posthumous

Reviews Misc. book reviews

Notes

Reprinted with permission from *Feminist Interpretations of Mary Wollstonecraft*, ed. Maria Falco (University Park, Pennsylvania: The Pennsylvania State University Press, 1996), 179–206.

1. Diana Coole, *Women in Political Theory: From Ancient Misogyny to Contemporary Feminism* (Brighton, Sussex: Wheatsheaf, 1988), 103.

Asking Questions about Women

My intent here is to show that in the conversation that is political theory, certain questions have been formulated and deemed to matter that do not reflect or incorporate feminist concerns and priorities. That is, nonfeminist political theorists not only differ from feminists in the answers they give but also in the questions they ask.

Here I introduce three texts in the history of feminist theory into the conversation to show how feminists explore gender issues, and how their approaches differ from those of texts in the history of nonfeminist theory. The contrasts are interesting and sometimes eye-opening, and provide some guidance for those committed to more inclusive theorizing.

Why didn't we know about these women? Was it possible that we were not meant to? And if women who raised their voices against male power became but a transitory entry in the historical records, what was to be the fate of the present women's movement? . . . I have come to accept that a patriarchal society depends in large measure on the experience and values of males being perceived as the *only* valid frame of reference for society, and that it is therefore in patriarchal interest to prevent women from sharing, establishing and asserting their equally real, valid and *different* frame of reference, which is the outcome of different experience.

Dale Spender, *Women of Ideas*

6

❦ ❦ ❦

Asking Questions about Women: Comparing Feminist and Nonfeminist Political Theorists

The idea for this essay, comparing the questions that feminist and nonfeminist theorists ask about women, has three sources. First, I often do things a little backward. For example, the only way I know how to subtract one number from another is to add the bottom two numbers together to get the top one. It also turned out that for me one effective way of reading political theory was to figure out what questions the writer was answering, explicitly or implicitly. It's a sort of *Jeopardy* approach to philosophy.[1]

Second, and more directly, I found myself uncomfortable with a commentary I read about Plato, which said something to the effect of "Well, he might not have had all the right answers on the subject of the status and relations of the sexes, but he asked the questions that continue to occupy feminists today." That struck me as not only untrue but also troubling. I looked at the rows and rows of books on my shelves on various aspects of feminism and thought, "No, he didn't talk about that, or that, or that." What troubled me was that there seemed to be more at stake in this than arguments about whether Plato was some sort of "protofeminist," although I don't mind proving along the way that he was not. What I thought the comment about Plato missed was the difference a feminist perspective makes in theorizing about gender. The historical contrasts in this essay are my attempt to show from another angle how differently feminists and nonfeminists (by which I mean to include consciously committed antifeminists as well as thoughtless ones) approach issues of gender.

There is a third motive, too. One of the points that feminist epistemologists and methodologists have been making is that mainstream political theory, like many (all?) other disciplines, is an exclusionary discourse. And they have generally meant by that not only that women (and often men with some trait deemed "minority" or "inferior") have been excluded from its theories as active subjects, which they certainly have been, but also that certain questions, perspectives, and concerns have been marginalized or rendered invisible. Comparing what questions feminist and nonfeminist political theorists have addressed or even raised on the subject of women is one of the ways of explaining that argument, even though it is not the only way and does not exhaust the scope of the claim.

In this chapter I will use Aristotle, Machiavelli, and Rousseau as nonfeminist theorists and Christine de Pizan, Mary Astell, and Mary Wollstonecraft as feminist theorists. These figures are from ancient, medieval, and modern political thought, from realist, Christian, and Enlightenment traditions, among the possible ways of classifying them (or pigeonholing them, or interpreting them as if there were one way to read them, depending upon your perspective). For each of these figures I will discuss the questions they ask regarding two general and definitely not comprehensive subjects: gendered (female and male) natures and male-female relationships.

One of the first problems in doing any of these comparisons is that most audiences have only read, and in some cases only heard of, the nonfeminist theorists. So I shall take a moment to introduce the feminists.

Christine de Pizan (ca. 1364–1429) wrote in the Middle Ages, which seemed less "dark" to me after discovering her. She was a most prolific writer, finishing some ten works in verse on subjects from love (*Le Debat de deux amans*) and a more perfect world (*Le Livre du chemin de long etude*) to history (*Le Livre de la Mutacion de Fortune*) and Joan of Arc (*Le Ditie de Jeanne d'Arc*). There were an additional eleven works in prose, one of which, *The Book of the City of Ladies*, written in 1405, I draw on in this essay.[2] It is an astonishing book, really, a text that erects a city in defense of women by responding to a wide range of popular, philosophical, literary, and historical arguments used to demean and subordinate women. She recovers and reassesses a history of women already largely lost even as she wrote half a millenium ago, and the fact that her most feminist book went without an English translation from 1521 to 1982 reminds us of how current the problem of erasure is. Even now I believe the only book on her as a political theorist is a recent anthology edited by Margaret Brabant, *Politics, Gender, & Genre: The Political Thought of Christine De Pizan* (Boulder, Colo.: Westview, 1992).

Mary Astell lived from 1668 to 1731. Writing around a hundred years before Mary Wollstonecraft, who is often wrongly called "the first feminist theorist," Astell's best-known works are *A Serious Proposal to the Ladies* (1694) and *Some Reflections upon Marriage Occasioned by the Duke and Duchess of Mazarine's Case* (1700). Astell writes with a mind in general and a wit in particular that is sharp, forthright, and satirical. She develops a concept of patriarchy, and an understanding of how it operates, that is a worthy foremother of contemporary treatment of the issue. Although often called a conservative thinker, a result of using male categories to label someone little captured by their confines, she would in many ways today be considered radical. As Dale Spender summarizes, "Both Astell and [Virginia] Woolf are acutely aware of the deficiencies and inadequacies in the way males have organised the world, and neither of them seeks for women simply a greater share of power in male-defined institutions."[3] Those interested in her are referred to one of only two books written about her, Ruth Perry's 1986 biography *The Celebrated Mary Astell* (always with women thinkers we have many times more biographies than treatments of them as theorists). Here I will draw primarily from Astell's *Reflections upon Marriage*.

Mary Wollstonecraft (1759–1797) is often the one feminist that theorists have heard of when they have heard of only one (what significance does that odd honor hold?). Nineteen ninety-two was the bicentennial of the publication of her most famous work, *A Vindication of the Rights of Woman*. Wollstonecraft, who lived only thirty-eight years, published a range of works on topics from the French Revolution (*A Vindication of the Rights of Men* and *Historical and Moral View of the Origin and Progress of the French Revolution*) to education (*Thoughts on the Education of Daughters*). She is often considered in one of two traditions: liberalism and feminism. Although she does deserve to be read within those, she should also be considered as a passionate voice for Enlightenment radicalism, a forerunner of nineteenth-century social attacks on property and class domination, a prose writer of some accomplishment, and an influential figure in the early development of romanticism.[4] As with the other women I consider here, there is only now a single and recent book on her political theory (the pattern is unmistakable), Virginia Sapiro's *A Vindication of Political Virtue: The Political Theory of Mary Wollstonecraft* (Chicago: University of Chicago Press, 1992). The works of hers I will use here are *A Vindication of the Rights of Woman* and her last, unfinished piece, *The Wrongs of Woman, or Maria*.

Gendered Natures

In attempting in his *Politics*[5] to characterize ("understand" hardly seems the right word) woman's nature Aristotle first asks whether by nature the female is like or unlike the slave (*Politics*, Book I, Ch. II). He then inquires into whether the slave, the child and the "wife" (not a woman, but a wife) have "any 'goodness' beyond that of discharging his function as an instrument and performing his menial service" (*Politics*, Book I, Ch. XIII)? For each of these groups he wonders whether all the parts of the soul, especially the 'higher' parts, are present in them, or, put another way, whether "the[ir] difference [from freemen] . . . is one of kind [or] . . . degree" (*Politics*, Book I, Ch. XIII)? Finally, he asks the related questions of whether women too have virtues: "Can [women] . . . be 'good', in the sense of temperate, and brave, and just?" (*Politics*, Book I, Ch. XIII). And, if women have moral virtue, are they "the same in a woman as they are in a man"? Is "the goodness of those who naturally rule the same as the goodness of those who are naturally ruled" (*Politics*, Book I, Ch. XIII)?

Aristotle's inquiry takes as an unexamined assumption that woman's nature is distinct from that of man. Actually, it's a little more complicated than that, because he doesn't simply speak of "men vs. women." Interestingly, his discussion of women takes place in the same sections as those addressing status as free or enslaved and as child or adult. His division is not just between men and women, then, but free men, citizen women, male and female children, and male and female slaves. Distinctions between male and female slaves and between male and female children are given less attention than the differences between all of them and free men. Class and gender, then, are both used inconsistently as meaningful divisions of people, a result of the fact that the privileged are privileged by virtue of being simultaneously adult, male, and free.

Regarding citizen women, which is the only group of females Aristotle singles out for attention, he does indeed begin with the assumption that woman's nature is different from man's. However, his discussion of men's nature generally discusses only how men are differentiated from non-humans—whatever is distinctively human is also male. Difference within the human species only is an issue once women enter the conversation, revealing an androcentricity we will shortly see again.

For Aristotle, citizen woman needs not only to be measured against the free and fully human male, but perhaps even more importantly to be considered in comparison to other "defective" humans: children and slaves. And here the questions seem more aimed at wondering whether there is anything that possibly positively distinguishes these women from other subordinated groups, than at challenging assumptions that lump them all together or differentiate any of them from the free male. His question about whether women might have any excellence beyond and higher than merely instrumental and ministerial qualities already presupposes that *some* people—male ones—are ends, for which others—children, slaves, citizen women—might be means. His questions lead us to understand that for Aristotle these subordinated groups are defined almost entirely by how they measure up to the male ruler, "ruler" being meant as both lord and measuring stick.

In investigating (again the word must be used loosely) woman's nature, Aristotle asks whether there may be exceptions, some "departure[s] from nature [which establishes that] . . . [t]he male is naturally fitter to command than the female" (*Politics*, Book I, Ch. XII)? Allowing the possibility that there is, he does not, however, inquire into the fate of these "exceptional women" in his theory or in his politics, nor does he ask what these exceptional women mean for theories—including his own—about the supposed polarity of sex differences.

Machiavelli's questions regarding gendered natures assume not only that they are different, but also oppositional. This conflict between them is captured in two questions that pervade his work. For men he wonders, how can we preserve the male ambition, the manly energy, that leads to political power, but also prevent it from turning into a self-defeating, insatiable hunger for power after power? For women he inquires, how do we restrain the influence of the feminine, which is associated with and symbolized by various forms of ingratitude, avarice, suspicion, envy, fickleness, and ambition?

Machiavelli's questions assume rather than inquire into whether there are sex differences. He seems to ask Aristotle-like questions of whether male ambition and male hunger for power are the same in any way as female ambition and female hunger for power, and he gives male ambition the kind of blessing of superiority Aristotle gave male rationality. That accomplished, his questions turn to what men of different positions have to watch out for in women of different ages and positions—what threats various women pose to various men.

Rousseau's treatment of women begins with two fundamental questions. First, what are "the similarities and the differences of her sex and ours" (*Emile*, 357);[6] and second, what is "the constitution of [woman's] species and her sex . . . [that allows her] to fill her place in the physical and moral order" (*Emile*, 357)?

Rousseau's two questions frame his discussion in peculiar ways.

In asking about "the similarities and the differences" between "her sex and ours," Rousseau makes clear his male-centeredness, his male audience, his use of the male as the norm.[7] And like Aristotle, he does not begin his discussion of male education by asking in what ways men differ from and resemble women, but treats males in isolation and then asks how women compare. Second, Rousseau's question about women's "place in the physical and moral order" comes in the next several pages to be reformulated as "After having tried to form the natural man, . . . how [should] the woman who suits this man . . . be formed" (*Emile,* 363)? Again like Aristotle, who assumes men's lives are ends in themselves but that women's might be instrumental for others, Rousseau first establishes the natural man and then turns to the woman "who suits this man." Having satisfied himself that women should have a distinctive function in the general scheme of things and in relation to men, Rousseau next asks: since "man and woman are not and ought not to be constituted in the same way in either character or temperament, . . . [should] they have the same education" (*Emile,* 363)? Concluding that they should not, he then asks, how can we best educate girls for adult lives in which they will "tame all their caprices in order to submit them to the will of others" (*Emile,* 369) and which "do not permit them to indulge themselves in any preferred talent to the prejudice of their duties" (*Emile,* 368)?

Rousseau's other questions about women's nature inquire into why any would think "it matter[s] that this or that woman produces few children . . . [when] women's status . . . [is none the] less that of motherhood" (*Emile,* 362)? He thus gives the same short shrift to "exceptional" or "unconventional" women that Aristotle did. He asks not whether women are capable of other things than being mothers, but how anyone could suppose that woman could "be nurse today and warrior tomorrow?" (*Emile,* 362). This question allows that women have potential to succeed at tasks outside their traditional ones, but also makes clear that any advocate of nontraditional roles has the burden of proving the compatibility of those tasks with traditional ones, a powerful slant.

Regarding virtue, Rousseau follows the pattern of asking, how are men's "failings" women's "good qualities" (*Emile,* 363)? How is women's "weakness" her "glory" (*Emile*, 360)? And what is note-worthy here is that regarding educating the sexes the same, Rous-seau's question is, how will training women "to resemble" men actually disempower women (*Emile*, 363, 364)? Or, what "abuses" will result from placing "the two sexes in the same employments and in the same labors" (*Emile*, 363)? His whole inquiry seems to be to figure out two things: first, how can the sexes be rendered "to act in concert" without doing "the same things". How can "the goal of their labors [be] . . . common, but their labors themselves . . . different, and consequently . . . the tastes directing them" (*Emile*, 363)? Second, how can this difference be understood and marketed as being in the interest of both sexes?

Rousseau is so absolutely clear about the fact that there are molds into which the sexes must be fit, molds that could be otherwise than they are, molds that require vigilant surveillance, that what he seems to be inquiring into is *not* what men are like or, even more obviously, *not* what women are like. His inquiry is how to educate each sex so that together they will be in a position to solve problems that Rousseau, not either of them, has named.

Christine de Pizan turns many of the questions nonfeminists ask about women on their head. Two questions establish her approach. First, she asks at the outset, "How [has] it happened that so many different men—and learned men among them—have been and are so inclined to express both in speaking and in their treatises and writings so many wicked insults about women and their behav-ior?" (*City of Ladies*, 3–4). "[T]ell me," she says, "if Nature makes man so inclined or whether they do it out of hatred and where does this behavior come from?" (*City of Ladies*, 16). De Pizan's book opens, in other words, with the possibility of something being wrong with *men's* nature rather than with women's, with the need for an account of men's behavior and deeds, rather than of wom-en's, and with an assumption that what has been said of woman's nature by men is questionable.

The second framing question of de Pizan's work is, how can it be that God "[n]ever created anything which was not good" yet woman was said to be "the vessel as well as the refuge and abode of every evil and vice" (*City of Ladies*, 5)? This question reveals a religious approach, or confrontation, or at least use of religion in women's name, including the use of God as an authority against "learned men" who demean women.

De Pizan's whole book is essentially a series of questions, much like Aquinas in this respect. But she doesn't ask Aquinas' question, "Whether the woman should have been made in the first production of things?" (*Summa Theologica*, Vol. 13, Part I, Question 92). Instead, her questions take the form of asking how we can respond to a certain insult men have hurled at women. She asks, for example, what we can say to those who claim "that women do not have a natural sense for politics and government" (*City of Ladies*, 32), or "that women have weak bodies . . . and are cowards by nature" (*City of Ladies*, 36).

Woman's nature then, is very much contested from the outset, is precisely what de Pisan wants to open up, to reveal as full of possibilities and possessing a history that does justice to those possibilities in spite of women's experience of oppression. One of the things that is so exciting about de Pizan's *Book of the City of Ladies* is that she does not shy away from any question. She does not think there is a question that defenders of women cannot handle. In fact, she will ask the same question a number of ways so that she can have the opportunity to respond from a number of angles. For example, on the question of women's intellectual abilities de Pizan asks "whether . . . God . . . [has] honor[ed] the feminine sex with the privilege of the virtue of high understanding and great learning, and whether women ever have a clever enough mind for this" (*City of Ladies*, 63). She then moves from the issue of "higher" intellectual function in the abstract to the question of why women in fact haven't achieved more than they have relative to men: "[S]ince they have minds skilled in conceptualizing and learning, just like men, why don't women learn more?" (*City of Ladies*, 63). She next asks about a more specific aspect of intellectual ability, whether women's intellect includes the ability to invent, or to discover anew rather than apply the old.

I realize that you are able to cite numerous and frequent cases of women learned in the sciences and the arts. But I would then ask you whether you know of any women who, through the strength of emotion and of subtlety of mind and comprehension, have themselves discovered any new arts and sciences which are necessary, good, and profitable, and which had hitherto not been discovered or known. (*City of Ladies*, 70–1)

Lest there still be doubts, she then moves on from the issue of abstract intellect to that of practical reason, asking "whether a woman's mind . . . is equally prompt and clever in those matters which prudence teaches, that is, whether women can reflect on what is best to do and what is better to be avoided?" (*City of Ladies*, 87).

De Pizan is a woman who believes that asking questions about women is part of the answer to women's oppression, who knows that unasked questions will be used against women. The range of subjects she explores and the depth with which each is treated contrast sharply with the narrow scope and superficial treatment of issues regarding gendered natures by nonfeminist theorists.

Mary Astell's discussion of female and male natures are framed within a broad question: How does the power of men distort their view of women (*Marriage*, 110, 111)? How does it distort their self-perceptions (*Marriage*, 119)? From there, she asks less often what is woman or what is man, but instead turns to questions about the consequences of men and women existing in certain ways. For example, she asks what are the peculiar consequences of "Pride and Self-conceit" in a husband vs. a wife (*Marriage*, 103–4)? The tendency to investigate real-world consequences *for women* of various gendered conditions is a hallmark of feminist theorizing about gender. It contrasts with a nonfeminist readiness merely to assert that this is all for women's own good, or to explore gendered conditions only as their consequences touch men or the supposedly common good which tends to exclude women's well-being.

Astell's treatment of the idea of woman as by nature goddess or madonna is a very political one. She asks, not of its truth, which she seems to say is not worth a response, but of its political consequences: what are the effects of speaking about women as if they were "Exemplary" and "having no faults" (*Marriage*, 99); what is the connection between praise for women in words and contempt for women in practice (*Marriage*, 100)?

It is not exact to say that Astell did not think the sexes different. Her project, however, was to inquire into the causes and the consequences of those differences—whether the differences tended to show women favorably or unfavorably—within an understanding of male power over women rather than by appeals to nature or to God or to women's faults. Many "explanations" of women's subordination become Astell's questions, much as was the case for de Pisan. And how much changes once this foundational issue is raised is part of the feminist challenge to political theory.

Wollstonecraft does not ask Aristotle's question of whether women's moral virtues are the same as those of men, or Rousseau's question of how the separate virtues of the sexes serve both individuals and communities well. Instead she asks two other questions. First, she wants to know how ideas of separate male and female virtues do not lead to a relativism that most who support such differentiated natures oppose? Second, she asks how women are "degraded by mistaken notions of female excellence" (*Rights*, 43)? This is a most interesting contrast and response to Aristotle, for his very concept of an excellence is as a perfection of something, and what Wollstonecraft does is to raise the possibility that what he and others call women's excellence actually degrades and debases women. Another way she asks the same questions but with a more obvious political twist (and one aimed at Rousseau) is, what ends are served by making "all the virtue of women consist in chastity, submission, and the forgiveness of injuries" (*Maria*, 214)? She challenges the idea of separate virtues yet another way, by asking whether the "masculine women" exclaimed against are women exhibiting male vices or human virtues (*Rights*, 41, 43). And finally on the subject of virtue, Wollstonecraft asks questions that attempt to reveal the inconsistency of patriarchal characterizations of women: how can it be that woman's superior intuition and sensibility are supposed to grant her a moral and spiritual excellence; yet *at the same time* her deficient reason and poor cognitive ability are supposed to preclude the possibility of stable moral character?[8]

Like most feminist theorists, Wollstonecraft's questions about what women and men are like is framed by an understanding of the influences of male power on what is called nature. She really begins her treatise advocating women's education by asking what sort of woman a system of unequal education is geared to produce, and what sort of woman it is incapable of producing (*Rights*, 40). Or put another way, she asks, if women are to be granted full moral responsibility, what kind of education must they have? Wollstonecraft is less engaged than is de Pisan in the task of reassessing both male and female roles and traits. But like Astell she does not shy away from what are considered unflattering characterizations of women, using them as an opportunity to raise questions that allow her the possibility of explaining their origins in patriarchy. For example, Wollstonecraft asks, what in women's training prevents women from rebelling against their reduction to "alluring objects" (*Rights*, 41, 42)? More generally, in her words, what "follies and caprices of [the female] sex . . . [are] the natural effect of ignorance (*Rights*, 44)? Perhaps most insightfully from the perspective of grappling with the variety of consequences of oppression, Wollstonecraft wants to know what are "the spirit-grinding consequences[s] of poverty and infamy" (*Maria*, 204, 206), and how does oppression turn the oppressed into "monster[s]" (*Maria*, 207)?

Male-Female Relations

In discussing the relationship between men and women in the family, Aristotle first asks whether the rule of the man in the household over the woman most resembles the rule of a statesman over citizens, of a king over subjects, a freeman over slaves, or a father over his children. In making such comparisons he asks which of these forms of rule is better, but he means which is better for the ruler; that is, are free men more ennobled by ruling over beasts, slaves, citizens or women? He does actually ask a related question about which is better for women, but it is phrased as whether it is "expedient and right" for women, *as inferiors*, to be ruled by men, to rule themselves, or to rule with men as equals. In seeking to justify male rule he first asks whether men rule women because of their superior physical force or their superiority in virtue, questions which reveal that male superiority itself is not subjected to doubt.

There is for Aristotle really no possibility that male-female relations exist outside of a hierarchy that gives one authority over the other. The question posed is what other hierarchy the hierarchy between the sexes most resembles, so that the form of rule used over women can be determined. This approach uses non-women to determine relations with women, a tactic vaguely reminiscent of Plato asking whether the difference between men and women is like or unlike that between bald-headed men and men with hair, as if women themselves were incapable of being accurate sources of information about themselves. In deciding which hierarchy the male-female hierarchy resembles, the questions Aristotle asks concern what form of rule over women would be good for men at least as much, and probably more, than what form of being ruled most elevates women.

Machiavelli's discussion of male-female relations is utterly dominated by concerns about restraining women. He asks, for example, how men can prevent women, love, and sexuality from depoliticizing them, from turning men away from politics to the private, and fragmenting the community? In another variety on the same theme he asks, with what powers, what masculine discipline and ferocity, can the female be countered and controlled? Men, of course, do also need to be restrained, primarily from women, and so he wonders, for example, how can we keep men, especially male rulers, from seizing women who are the property of other men, thereby stirring up opposition and internal division? The "even-handedness" of these questions rest in that for both sexes in the male-female relationship constraint is part of where they meet. Men, however, are to control themselves from the power women might exert over them, while women are to be controlled by men lest women get too powerful. Men's self-control is really part of empowering men, while control of women is also part of empowering men.

Machiavelli does not really ask whether the two sexes can be *harmonized* through male rule, as does Aristotle, but his question of whether men can *control* women's influence on males and the political community is not so different from Aristotle's in its focus on how women must be ruled in the name of male-defined politics. Machiavelli's questions assume, more than Aristotle's do, that women do in fact have power of some sorts over men, a difference likely due to the fact that Aristotle envisions males as more ruled by their reason and Machiavelli by their appetites, although for both women's power is undesirable and needs to be contained.

Rousseau's discussion of women is in fact dominated by questions about women's proper and improper relationships with men. Within that framework he tends to assume, like both Aristotle and Machiavelli, that a power relationship between the sexes is necessary, and his concern is which kind of power each sex should rightly exert over the other. He asks, for example, "If woman is made to please and to be subjugated, [should] she . . . make herself agreeable to man [or] . . . arousing" (*Emile*, 358)? This is a loaded question, to say the least, but what he is asking is which form of power women subordinated to men in certain ways should exert back over men: will they gain more by being agreeable or arousing? So the question is loaded, but in a somewhat different way than we sometimes think about it. Rousseau is assuming that we should ask questions about relationships from an understanding of them as based on "attack and defense" (*Emile*, 358). And lest anyone think him unfair in this, he pleadingly asks, "Is it our fault that they [women] please us when they are pretty, that their mincing ways seduce us, that the art which they learn from you attracts us and pleases us, that we like to see them tastefully dressed, that we let them sharpen at their leisure the weapons with which they subjugate us?" (*Emile*, 363).

De Pizan turns to male-female relationships with the same determination to ask any question—a desire she showed on the subject of gendered natures—to which a response might be made to opponents of women's equality. She begins her inquiry challenging a patriarchal characterization of marriage as really in women's interests and against those of men. She asks whether it "is true . . . that life within the institution of marriage is filled and occupied with such great unhappiness for men because of women's faults and impetuosity, and because of their rancorous ill-humor, as is written in so many books?" (*City of Ladies*, 118). She turns next to inquire into the truth of the accusation that "women hate their husbands when they are old and also that women do not love men of learning or scholars, for he claims the duties entailed in the upkeep of women are totally incompatible with the study of books" (*City of Ladies*, 128). She also investigates more specific claims that affect recommendations of proper female-male relations, such as whether "a man should not tell his wife anything which he wishes to conceal [because] . . . women are unable to be silent" (*City of Ladies*, 134), whether it is true that "men who believe or lend credence to their wives' advice are despicable and foolish" (*City of Ladies*, 137), and what to think of "the opinion of some men who claim that they do not want their daughters, wives, or kinswomen to be educated because their mores would be ruined as a result" (*City of Ladies*, 153). De Pizan raises questions about whether it is true that there are "few chaste women" (*City of Ladies*, 155) and then whether there few beautiful and chaste women (*City of Ladies*, 158)! It is as if she does not want a reader to be able to say, "Okay, Christine answered one question, but not this particular twist on it." Lest too many of these examples, or the language in which they are expressed, sound quaint and outdated, de Pizan also asks about the "argu[ment] that many women want to be raped and that it does not bother them at all to be raped by men even when they verbally protest" (*City of Ladies*, 161) and about how we explain why women "suffered so long without protesting against the horrors charged by different men when they knew that these men were greatly mistaken" (*City of Ladies*, 185). And in many of these inquiries she also asks where the wrong ideas about women come from, and what the consequences are of righting and failing to right those wrong ideas, questions that allow her to look into the structures of male power and the realities of women's daily lives.

In looking at female-male relations Mary Astell's primary task is to answer, what are the consequences and dangers of "unequal Marriage" (*Marriage*, 90)? She first inquires into the daily realities for a woman of living with a husband who is her "absolute Lord and Master" (*Marriage*, 90, 102, 105). She asks, perhaps most importantly for many of her opponents, what we learn from transferring or applying the arguments against arbitrary power in government to the power of men in marriage (*Marriage*, 102, 111). She brings a political analysis to bear on questions such as what factors make violence against and disregard for women in marriage more and less likely (*Marriage*, 106), and, related, what makes the power of the husband so liable to abuse. She wonders whether men's power can be restrained, and whether it can be exercised for good.

Where she talks about male-female relations, which is obviously the subject of her treatise on marriage, Astell explores how male power corrupts marriage even as it serves male interests, an important feminist distinction between the partial interests of privilege and the interests of a differently constituted whole. She wants to know what the realities of marriage are for women, and what the social functions are of romantic love.

Wollstonecraft's look at marriage includes inquiry into questions such as: what does it mean for a woman to be refused access to divorce? And what does it mean for a woman to be married to a superior (*Maria*, 211–215)? Outside of marriage, Wollstonefcaft asks in *Maria* what are the "equally oppressive . . . [but different] wrongs of different classes of women" in various relationships with men (196)? Rather than simply accepting what men have written about the power they feel women have over them, Wollstonecraft asks exactly what the power of women to "excite desire" means for their relationships with men (*Rights*, 43), and what the effects are for women of "the great art of pleasing" (*Rights*, 50). She wants as well to question the ideal of marriage, asking what is wrong with the argument that "in order to make a man and his wife *one*, that she should rely entirely on his understanding," (*Rights*, 46), a question which shows that Wollstonecraft not only challenges Rousseau's understanding of gender relations, but also Aristotle's.

Conclusions

It may not be far-fetched to conclude that antifeminists and non-feminists ask all the wrong questions about women and feminists all the right ones. Further, the feminist theorists I have used above help explain why it is more likely to be that way than not, a political explanation that is shrewd in its understanding of the forms and abuses of power and privilege.

But the first conclusion I want to draw is that it is important to see that all of the writers considered here are political in their discussions of women, and not only the feminist ones. They all understand the possible impact, for example, of various relationships between the sexes on politics, and thus base their endorsement of certain forms of marital power structures on political considerations. They most obviously differ in what they consider political ends worth working towards—Aristotle is willing to domesticate citizen women and enslave women and men so that a certain ideal of male citizenship can be fulfilled, while Wollstonecraft is willing to urge equality between husband and wife so that children will have a model of democracy to take with them into the political world—but that difference does not make one "political" and the other "neutral" or "objective" or "disinterested." Even more strongly, when we look at the questions that nonfeminists refused to ask, it is hard to resist concluding that it is the nonfeminists who are aligned with partial interests, who shun "seeing" certain things, who are political in the avoidably negative rather than merely inevitable sense of the word.

A second interesting conclusion to be drawn from this study is that however much we have made of the distinctions between malestream philosophers—between idealists and empiricists, between Enlightenment and Romantic theorists, between medievalists and modernists—antifeminism also links them, exists as a common if hidden ground that contrasts with their often-talked about differences. And there is a different common ground among the feminist thinkers, which is that whatever tradition they wrote in or in response to, they were belittled and deemed unworthy of much serious response or analysis.

One final issue. Which came first: the biased question or the biased answer? Did Aristotle not ask certain questions because they would not lead to his predetermined answers, or did the fact that he did not ask certain questions lead to the answers he offers? I'm not sure this is answerable, although I would guess that if it is answerable that the answer is that the answers came first. But ultimately, that is not what really matters. What matters is the knowledge that without asking certain questions certain answers can look right that are brought into question through other questions. I tell my children and my students that learning to ask good questions is more important than being able to answer them. This project has reaffirmed my conviction in the truth of that statement, for it shows how much more damage can be done by ceasing to raise questions than by raising them and answering them even incompletely or inaccurately. For asking them renders the inquiry legitimate even if people disagree with the answers offered, while not asking them makes certain problems invisible if not illegitimate.

The feminists treated here did not, however, ask all of the questions that feminists today are asking, and no doubt we today are not asking all of the questions that will occupy feminists a hundred years from now. Nonetheless, there definitely is a distinctive feminist tradition, a history of feminist theory, that links thinkers across the centuries, across national boundaries, sometimes even across class, sexual, and racial divides. It is a history both worth knowing and worth building upon.

Notes

1. It's hard to resist the temptation of devising a whole program here! The *Jeopardy* categories for our contest would be interesting: "Sexism in Philosophy for $500, Alex." But the negative is so overwhelming it conquers the desire to be clever. Too much is really "at risk" in this discussion. And what could possibly constitute "double jeopardy" and "final jeopardy" given the norm of risk entailed in being female in a patriarchal culture?

2. I draw here on Marina Warner's foreword to Earl Richards' translation of *The Book of the City of Ladies* (New York: Persea Books, 1982), xiii–li.

3. Dale Spender, *Women of Ideas and What Men Have Done to Them* (Winchester, Mass.: Pandora, Unwin Hyman, 1982), 59.

4. I learned some of this from valuable conversations and paper exchanges with Berenice Carroll.

5. I am using Ernest Barker's translation, *The Politics of Aristotle* (Oxford University Press, 1975).

6. All references here are to Rousseau's *Emile, or On Education*, translated by Allan Bloom (New York: Basic Books, 1979). Page references are placed in the text.

7. Nanerl Keohane also makes this point in " 'But for Her Sex . . .': The Domestication of Sophie," *University of Ottawa Quarterly* 49 (July 1979), 394.

8. Carolyn N. Korsmeyer, "Reason and Morals in the Early Feminist Movement: Mary Wollstonecraft," in *Women and Philosophy: Toward a Theory of Liberation*, ed. Carol C. Gould and Marx W. Wartofsky (New York: Putnam's, 1976), 105.

Feminism and Communitarianism

I wrote this as someone strongly committed to certain forms of community who could not understand why communitarians were so uninterested in feminism. In grappling with why various communitarian texts seemed to espouse patriarchal values, even as they renounced the patriarchal principles of liberalism, I came to compare their reasons for rejecting liberalism with feminism's critique of liberalism. Putting the two literally side by side in this text, both the common ground and the differences between feminism and communitarianism become obvious, and the dialogue each has with liberalism is also visible.

Probably the most obvious thing about what makes this community a community is that it is *not* that we agree on everything. There is, in fact, much disagreement on practically everything. . . . So what *is* there? What holds us in community? . . . What I'm getting at here is that it's the natural normal thing for women to be connected and sustained in community with each other, and it has nothing in particular to do with agreeing about anything, or even liking each other. It certainly doesn't have anything in particular to do with approving of each other. Instead of looking for something like common values to account for what holds us together, we should consider whatever kept us apart or works to keep us apart.

Marilyn Frye, "Lesbian Community"

7

🌿 🌿 🌿

Feminism and Communitarianism: Comparing Critiques of Liberalism

Why, when there is so much interest in community among feminists, is there so little interest in feminism among communitarians? In terms of their philosophical assumptions and political ideals, there exists enough common ground between feminism and communitarianism that the cool relationship between them is somewhat curious. Both emphasize context, care, and community, and both reject central features of liberalism. Yet from Plato to Sandel communitarians display, at best, an aloofness from the issues that inform feminism, and today some feminists explicitly warn against alliances with communitarians. It seems that whatever the extent to which communitarian theorists might be said to be egalitarian, inegalitarian threads also connect them—threads that, variously throughout history, define women out of certain communities, downplay the negative effects of women's domestication, exclude women in conceptions and calculations of the "common" good, refuse to address sexual differentiation and inequality as obstacles to personal and political bonds, and advocate patriarchal principles, values, and structures to guide their communities.

To understand why feminists and communitarians have not been, are not, and perhaps cannot or should not be more consistent allies,

I compare the contemporary feminist and communitarian critiques of liberalism's conceptions of the self, social relations, and political community. Regarding each of these, I consider central aspects of: (a) how communitarians and feminists understand the liberal view, (b) what each finds problematic in it and, at least briefly, (c) what alternatives each endorses.

It is important to see precisely where (nonfeminist) communitarians diverge from (even communitarian) feminists. I argue here that contemporary communitarians fail to offer a critique of liberalism that gives voice to concerns heard in feminist critiques of liberalism, even when those feminist critiques are informed by a commitment to community. Feminists thus cannot "choose" between alignment with liberals or with communitarians, cannot choose one side of an old battle in which women's interests, at best, are secondary. Instead, we need to reconfigure the recurring debate between liberals and communitarians into one that includes what might be called communitarian feminism, or, perhaps better, the communitarian strain of numerous feminists. For feminism challenges the terms of both liberalism and communitarianism in ways that neither does of the other.

While both communitarianism and feminism are almost astonishingly diverse in theory and practice, focusing only on their critiques of liberalism allows me to talk about each in something resembling a generic form. I treat writings by a number of feminist and communitarian thinkers without attempting systematically to analyze any particular individual, since my aim is more general. Nor does it matter whether these feminists and communitarians have perceived liberalism correctly, whatever that might mean. In fact, several writers contend that aspects of liberalism criticized by feminists and communitarians are not integral to liberalism. For the purpose of understanding where feminism and communitarianism part ways, what matters is their perceptions of liberalism and its limitations.

Not all feminists are strong communitarians. Feminist opposition to community exists, for example, among liberal feminists wary of politicizing the private out of fear of government power, among postmodern feminists wary of the fate and status of differences in a unified community, and among those feminists dissatisfied with facile glorification of "the feminine" as a model of community. Even among feminists committed to community debate is ongoing, including, for example, questions about how much feminists can or should adopt from traditional women's communities and about what practices and structures nurture both community and individuality.

The warnings issued by feminists about community (which, to avoid confusion, are distinct from warnings about feminist alliance with nonfeminist communitarianism) are valid and important to address. But all feminisms, including liberal feminism, challenge aspects of classic liberalism from a position that is less individualistic and more communitarian than classical liberalism,[1] and of concern here are the grounds on which feminism does challenge liberalism. Despite the fact that there are feminist visions very much more and less informed by community, generic feminism, or "feminism unmodified," still opposes central ideas and practices of classic liberalism. Yet the critiques of liberalism by contemporary communitarians and feminists are not based upon and do not lead to similar understandings or visions of politics.

Conceptions of the Self

Understanding Liberalism

Communitarianism

The dispute between communitarians and liberals hinges on opposing conceptions of the self. Where liberals conceive of the self as essentially unencumbered and free to choose among a wide range of alternatives, communitarians insist that the self is situated in and constituted by tradition, membership in a historically rooted community.[2]

[For liberals] Individuals . . . are primary and society secondary, and the identification of individual interests

Feminism

Abstract individualism considers individual human beings as social atoms, abstracted from their social contexts, and disregards the role of social relationships and human community in constituting the very identity and nature of individual human beings.[5]

Although it would be mistaken to suggest that all liberal theorists conceive of human nature as being egoistic, most do argue that people tend naturally in this direction and must

is prior to, and independent of, the construction of any moral or social bonds between them.[3]

[Liberalism's] atomism posits that as physical beings, humans are separate, integral, self-contained, unitary particles or atoms.[4]

work to develop moral capacities to counter their basic selfish, acquisitive inclinations.[6]

[Abstract individualism is] the assumption that the essential human characteristics are properties of individuals and are given independently of any particular social context. . . . [It] takes human nature as a presocial system.[7]

Both feminists and communitarians find in liberalism the notion of a presocial, solitary subject with "natural" rights. Both see as a central feature of liberalism its belief that individual interests exist before or independent of social relationships, moral bonds, a social context, or the human community. Liberalism, it is said, views individual selves as having identities apart from their ends. The liberal self is also one who can and should be free—an individual whose relations, attachments, and goals are chosen from a wide range of alternatives and are detachable, independent of the self.[8] Liberal theory starts with the individual outside of society, fully developed, in possession of "natural" rights and duties, and unable to live very well with other basically self-concerned individuals, the guidance of "natural" law notwithstanding.

To the extent that the independent self of liberalism is given content, the substance is in terms of tendencies, motivations, and capacities. The individual of liberal theory is thought, for example, to tend to be self-interested; to be motivated by profit, pleasure, and pride; and to be capable of rationality, usually equated with prudential reasoning. That toward which one moves is undetermined: what gives pleasure, what profits, and what inspires one to reason instrumentally are individual variables and not essential or social features.

While contemporary feminist and communitarian understandings of liberalism's view of the self have much in common with each other, and while it may be "a commonplace amongst communitarians, socialists and feminists that liberalism is to be rejected for its excessive 'individualism' or 'atomism' " (Kymlicka 181), their grounds for rejecting it are not identical. And this is true despite the fact that each understands the implications of their critique to undercut everything from the liberal conception of freedom as non-interference to the liberal justification of the state as fulfilling the interests of its citizens.

Critiques of the Liberal View

Communitarianism

[For the] right to exist prior to the good it would be necessary for the subject to exist independently of his/her intentions and his/her ends. Such a conception requires therefore a subject who can have an identity defined prior to the values and objectives that he/she chooses. It is, in effect, the capacity to choose, not the choices that he makes, that defines such a subject. He can never have ends which are constitutive of his identity and this denies him the possibility of participation in a community where it is the very definition of who he is that is in question.[9]

[T]he peculiarly modern self, the emotivist self, in acquiring sovereignty in its own realm lost its traditional boundaries provided by a social identity and a view of human life as ordered to a given end. (MacIntyre 32)

Feminism

Feminist theorists argue that the vision of the atomic, "unencumbered self," criticized by communitarians, is a male one, since the degree of separateness and independence it postulates among individuals has never been the case for women. . . . Indeed, her individuality has been sacrificed to the "constitutive definitions" of her identity. . . . If unencumbered males have difficulties in recognizing those social relations constitutive of their ego identity, situated females often find it impossible to recognize their true selves amidst the constitutive roles that attach to their persons.[10]

[A]t each moment of our lives our every thought, value, and act—from the most mundane to the most lofty—takes its meaning and purpose from the wider political and social reality that constitutes and conditions us. (Dietz 1)

Communitarians and feminists both reject the liberal notion of an isolated self with rights, interests, values, and ends independent of a social context. They do so, however, for different reasons. I discuss three differences in the communitarian and feminist critiques of liberalism's conception of the self, looking both to describe the differences and to give some account of their origins and implications. The three differences concern sources of identity, the extent of socialization, and evaluations of traditional societies.

First, in discussing the range of social forces that influence the formation of the self, Sandel talks of the "family or community or nation or people,"[11] and MacIntyre includes families, neighborhoods, cities, guilds, professions, clans, tribes, and nations (MacIntyre 204–5). The factors left out of such accounts are often precisely the ones with which feminists are critically concerned. From a feminist perspective, most centrally affecting the formation of the self are factors such as sex, age, race, sexuality, and class. Yet about such things most nonfeminist communitarians are peculiarly hushed. Despite communitarian interest in "traditions" and "practices," their notion of social context seems to be somewhat narrowly conceived. While including certain well-defined groups and communities, it omits such traditions and practices as sexism and racism, practices that may have a larger role in forming the self and determining one's social place than do cities or neighborhoods, not least because the former are more pervasive, constant, intimate, and unconscious. Such forces as sexism and homophobia, for example, not only often create distinct communities ("the lesbian community," Boy Scouts, etc.) but also establish relations that pervade and structure all communities, including ones that seem to have nothing to do with gender, race, sexuality, or class.

According to feminists, communitarian language and theory are falsely universalized; communitarians challenge liberalism's pronouncements without noting how their accuracy varies according to the race, class, gender, or sexuality of individuals and groups. Without attention to such factors it is difficult to assess the accuracy of liberalism's descriptions. For example, communitarians fail to note that the separated self of liberalism reflects the reality of men more than women. Liberalism's portrait may also be more reflective in many Western cultures of those who are white and/or heterosexual than of those who are Black and/or homosexual, for as oppressed minorities the latter have bound together in "subcultures." In the communitarian critique there is some wavering about whether the picture of the self drawn by liberalism is descriptively accurate but normatively undesirable, or both inaccurate and undesirable (see Walzer). Such wavering may be a consequence of a misguided attempt to universalize what sexism and other forces of social domination render incapable of universalization. Liberalism's descriptions of social identity are more apt in some areas than in others, and in most areas vary according to factors ignored by communitarians.

In their critiques of liberalism's view of the self feminists not only recognize a broader range of social forces that influence identities than do communitarians, but they also find that these forces have a deeper impact than is generally acknowledged by communitarians. For example, while communitarians are most likely to consider the social nature of individual interests and ends, feminists stress how social context affects everything from individual characteristics, emotions, beliefs, capacities, and motives to human nature itself.[12] This difference may be attributed to the fact that feminists have always had to engage in debate over whether women and men have different natures. Feminists from Christine de Pizan and Harriet Taylor to Simone de Beauvoir and bell hooks have understood the differences between the sexes to be caused at least in large part by their different social experiences, their different social contexts. It would seem that one of the earliest and most consistent sources of feminist rejection of abstract individualism is the understanding of how strongly desires, physiques, interests, values, emotions, and other traits depend on a social context, and how rejection of this truth historically led to lies about the natures of the sexes, lies that were claimed to provide evidence for the naturalness and inevitability of male supremacy. Perhaps, then, the absence of this political history is what permits communitarians to see the impact of social context as both narrower and shallower than it is seen by feminists.

A third difference in the feminist and communitarian critiques of liberalism's view of the self is the standpoint from which they are leveled. As the earlier quotes show, the contrast can sometimes be stark: communitarians are concerned with the *loss* of "traditional boundaries," while feminists are concerned with the *costs* of those boundaries, especially for women. Nostalgia for communities of the past almost forces nonfeminist communitarians to gloss over or ignore those social forces and structures that have allowed and justified exclusion, oppression, and hierarchy. Feminism's defining commitment to ending oppression directs it at precisely those structures and practices communitarianism so often denies or marginalizes.

The difference in standpoints does not mean that the communitarian critique is apolitical, as evidenced by MacIntyre's concern, for example, with social decay and dislocation. But communitarian criticism often remains politically vague and abstract. It is not clear, for example, who feels dislocated and why, and who, perhaps, does not. It could be the case, for example, that the women's movement and the Black civil rights movement have raised uncomfortable questions about "place" for white men and that the emergence of such questions contributes positively to society. The vagueness of the communitarian critique tends in practice to reinforce conservative, inegalitarian politics.

Alternatives to the Liberal View

Communitarianism

[I]t is through his or her membership in a variety of social groups that the individual identifies himself or herself and is identified by others. I am brother, cousin and grandson, member of this household, that village, this tribe. These are not characteristics that belong to human beings accidentally, to be stripped away in order to discover "the real me." They are part of my substance, defining partially at least and sometimes wholly my obligations and my duties. Individuals inherit a particular space within an interlocking set of social relationships; lacking that space, they are nobody, or at best a stranger or an outcast. (MacIntyre 32)

Feminism

[W]hereas communitarians emphasize the situatedness of the disembedded self in a network of relations and narratives, feminists also begin with the situated self but view the *renegotiation* or our psychosexual identities, and their *autonomous reconstitution* by individuals as essential to women's and human liberation. . . . The simple identification of the subject with its social roles reinstates the very logic of identity that feminists have sought to critique in their examinations of the psychosexual constitution of gender. (Benhabib and Cornell 12–13)

As may already be clear, what communitarians prefer to liberalism is an Aristotelian understanding of the self as fundamentally political, realizing itself only in a given historical setting, a particular social context. The Aristotelian understanding views the self as embedded in and constituted by particular communal commitments and values. It sees participation in a value-defining community as giving the self a conception of right and justice. It understands that by and large the forces that constitute one's self—family, nation, etc.—are outside of one's free choosing. Finally, this view is preferred by communitarianism because of its ability to "locate" people, to give them an identity that delineates their obligations and determines the contours of their relationships, thereby providing personal and political stability, limits, and order.

Feminists do not deny that "through his or her membership in a variety of social groups . . . the individual identifies himself or herself and is identified by others" (MacIntyre 32). It would be most surprising, even impossible, for those with the political understanding feminists have of gender "socialization" or "conditioning" (to use terms that for some reason sound almost quaint today) to think otherwise. To say that socialization, or embeddedness, is inevitable, however, is only a modest beginning. The process of identity formation within and between cultures takes a wide range of forms that lead to distinctly different ways of living and living together. Feminists are more interested than are communitarians in understanding *how* social selves are constituted, toward what ends, and with what costs and benefits for various individuals, groups, and relations. Given the experience of gender oppression, feminists are likely to work for understandings of the self that acknowledge human interdependence, social responsibility, and an end to "gender obsession." Further, knowledge of the historical reality of social change and the present need for it tempers a possible resignation by showing that the individual can constructively gain some distance from the community, can critique and evaluate, and can work to create alternative cultures that will foster individuals with new concepts of themselves and others. Such choice and critical distance are viewed differently by feminists and communitarians because of their different evaluations of how fragile and destructive bonds are perceived as being.

The political challenge made by feminists to abstract individualism rejects the communitarian vision. Liberalism's ideal is criticized for encouraging people to think of themselves first, for fostering egoism and rewarding selfishness, and for drawing a picture of the self that is incomplete where it is not inaccurate. But the complacent communitarian reliance on "place" and inattention to the *problems* of social identity are also rejected for failing to address, and therefore to solve, the issues at the heart of feminism.

Grounded in women's experiences, feminist argument does not see the self as so unconnected as to make individual autonomy dangerous, so rapacious as to make meeting material needs an impossible means for encouraging solidarity, or so asocial as to make chosen communities untenable.

Social Relations

Understanding Liberalism

Communitarianism

[According to liberalism] the social world [is] nothing but a meeting place for individual wills, each with its own set of attitudes and preferences, who understand that world solely as an arena for the achievement of their own satisfaction. (MacIntyre 24)

[T]he liberal portrait of human nature . . . construe[s] the human essence as radically individual and solitary, as hedonistic and prudential, and as social only to the extent required by the quest for preservation and liberty in an adversary world of scarcity. (Barber 213)

[For individualists] No binding obligations and no wider social understanding justify a relationship. It exists only as the expression of the choices of the free selves who make it up. And should it no longer meet their needs, it must end.[13]

Feminism

Western liberal democratic thought has been built on the concept of the "individual" seen as a theoretically isolatable entity. This entity can assert interests, have rights, and enter into contractual relations with other entities. But this individual is not seen as related to other individuals in inextricable or intrinsic ways. This individual is assumed to be motivated primarily by a desire to pursue his own interest, though he can recognize the need to agree to contractual restraints on the ways everyone may pursue their interests.[14]

According to both feminists and communitarians, the liberal vision of interpersonal relations follows from its atomism: the boundaries of human relations are drawn by the nature of the self, understood in liberalism as competitive, privatistic, hedonistic, prudential, isolated, and self-interested. Liberal assumptions theoretically limit the potential bonds that can and should be created between people to ones that are voluntary, self-interested, instrumental, and contractual. Parties to contracts, however, like their interests, remain essentially separate. According to feminist and communitarian portraits of liberal theory, people see themselves, rightly, not primarily as members of a group with a common good and shared values, but as individuals with independent identities and separate, often opposed interests. Relationships are more akin to "mere associations" than to full-fledged communities because they are based solely on "congruent private interests" and are not capable of progressing beyond this base (Buchanan 856–57). That social world which does exist is minimal, because the individual of liberal theory does not seem to want, to need, or to be able to form deep connections with others; in fact, in a world perceived to be in a condition of scarcity, others may even be enemies, clashing in what is aptly called the social "arena." Self-interest both forces individuals into a social setting and restricts how social that setting can be.

While there seems to be no significant difference in the communitarian and feminist understandings of the liberal view of social relationships, such harmony once again abruptly ends when they critique it. To the extent that it is true that "[t]he central issue for political theory is not the constitution of the self but the connection of constituted selves, the pattern of social relations" (Walzer 21), differences here may reflect fundamentally different political perspectives.

Critiques of the Liberal View

Communitarianism

[O]ur great modern free world is all too often a world in which men and women do not exist for others; . . . in which altruistic behavior is discouraged in the name of bargaining effi-

Feminism

To see contactual relations between self-interested or mutually disinterested individuals as constituting a paradigm of human relations is to take a certain historically specific con-

ciency and utility accounting. . . . In this world, there can be no fraternal feeling, no general will, no selfless act, no mutuality, no species identity, no gift relationship, no disinterested obligation, no social empathy, no love or belief or commitment that is not wholly private. (Barber 71–72)

Liberal theory . . . deprives us of any ready access to our own experience of communal embeddedness. . . . It explains our inability to form cohesive solidarities, stable movements and parties that might make our deep convictions visible and effective in the world. (Walzer 10)

ception of "economic man" as representative of humanity. And it is, many feminists are beginning to agree, to overlook or to discount in very fundamental ways the experience of women. . . . To the extent that some of our relations should be seen as contractual, we should recognize how essentially limited rather than general such relations are. (Held 113, 115)

Atomism cannot . . . represent non-peer relationships like those of parent and child, teacher and student, or any where one person takes care of the interest of another.[15]

Communitarians find at least two things troubling in the liberal account of human relations. First, because the relations between people are portrayed as superficial, extrinsic, and utilitarian, individuals remain essentially alone, private. Altruism, fraternity [sic], mutuality, and empathy are discouraged, penalized, or dissolved by liberal ideology and social and economic structures, while narrowly self-interested acts are encouraged and rewarded. Consequently, "[u]nder such conditions many individuals will be incapable of achieving genuine community, either because the pressures to live the life of an autonomous chooser of ends will undermine their own attempts at commitment, or because they will be unable to rely upon the commitments of others" (Buchanan 866). The loss or absence of community, whether caused by or reflected in the philosophy of liberalism, is seen as both real and regrettable.

A second, and generally incompatible, communitarian critique of the liberal approach to human relations recognizes within liberal societies the existence and especially the validity of nonvoluntary, noncontractual relations and obligations—familial, communal, and national—and faults liberalism for inadequately accounting for them. The problem with liberalism in this reading is not the actual absence of community but the theoretical misrepresentation or neglect of concrete communal experiences. The incompleteness of liberal theory affects action and understanding, leaving people with motives too weak to protect communities, models too meager to assist efforts in creating and maintaining communities, and doubts too serious about the trustworthiness and altruism of others to support communal political activism.

The differences between the feminist and communitarian critiques here seem to be ones of emphasis and specificity. While this sounds like a relatively minor divergence, the differences, when examined, reveal very distinct political agendas.

The stress in feminist analysis is on how very few actual relations the liberal account covers, rather than on the actual lack of noncompetitive, other-concerned, interdependent relations in society. Positive relations of dependency, of care, of cooperation, and between unequals all exist but are omitted in varying ways in the liberal account, despite the fact that these are relations in which we spend most of our lives: as children or parents, teachers or students, clients or helpers, employers or employees.

This criticism, which thus far is very similar to at least one strain of the communitarian commentary, is more precise in naming what and who is left out. Feminists argue that what liberal analysis most systematically neglects are the experiences of women and children and of the private realm with which they are primarily identified. Given the earlier feminist argument that the supposedly neutral, abstract individual of liberal theory is, to the extent there is reality to the model, a (privileged) male, it follows that the social relations of liberal theory are, to the extent they reflect reality, those between men or seen from a (privileged) male perspective. "If the epitome of what it is to be human is thought to be a disposition to be a rational contractor, human persons creating other human persons through the processes of human mothering are overlooked. And human children developing human personhood are not recognized as engaged in a most obviously human activity" (Held 120). The recognition this neglect generally receives from (nonfeminist) communitarians is minimal, and thus its importance is minimized: "it is an interesting question, *not addressed here*, whether this first [Marxist] communitarian critique speaks to the experience of women: Are necessity and private interest their only bonds with one another?" (Walzer 8; emphasis added).

Further, feminists point out that this omission of women, children, and the private is an "oversight" with real costs. For example, "it is a great distortion of the [traditional] place of married women to see them as self-interested, autonomous beings competing for the satisfaction of their interests. This way of viewing them will not lead to a recognition of the real needs such women have" (Wolgast 155–56).

This feminist attention to women's lives can be connected to another point made by feminists and not found, or not emphasized, in the communitarian literature. Not only is it argued that narrowly self-interested relations should be understood as one limited variety of human experience, but liberalism's very understanding of self-interest is challenged as too restricted: "when people think about what they want, they think about more than just their narrow self-interest. When they define their own interests and when they act to pursue those interests, they often give great weight both to their moral principles and to the interests of others."[16]

There is more in the communitarian critique that feminists find deeply troubling. In considering nonvoluntary, noncontractual relations, communitarians tend to speak of "the family" as a universal, unproblematical, and undifferentiated unit and to link it with political community and nation. By lumping the familial with the political, communitarians make it too easy to assume that the two do or should serve the same ends and consist of similar relationships. Yet analogies such as these have brought particular harm to women, by providing, for example, "evidence" of the need for a (male) head of household and by turning child rearing into the task of "republican motherhood." By neglecting to differentiate the relations *within* families, communitarians render invisible power differences correlated with age and gender, as well as many of the problems to which they contribute, including the numerous forms of domestic violence. By not discussing varieties of family structures across time and from culture to culture communitarians implicitly leave the heterosexual, patriarchal family as *the* norm. The family of communitarian theory is too often that which serves male advantage. Thus, while feminists, like communitarians, do take issue with liberalism for its neglect of the family, feminists are more interested in bringing the familial experiences of women and children into the conversation, and the attention they want paid to the family is far more critical.

Alternatives to Liberalism

Communitarianism

So to see ourselves as deontology would see us is to deprive us of these qualities of character, reflectiveness, and friendship that depend on the possibility of constitutive projects and attachments. And to see ourselves as given to commitments such as these is to admit a deeper commonality than benevolence describes, a commonality of shared self-understanding as well as "enlarged affection." As the independent self finds its limits in those aims and attachments from which it cannot stand apart, so justice finds its limits in those forms of community that engage the identity as well as the interests of the participants. (Sandel 181–82)

Feminism

Instead of importing into the household principles derived from the marketplace, perhaps we should export to the wider society the relations suitable for mothering persons and children . . . relations . . . characterized by more care and concern and openness and trust and human feeling than are the contractual bargains that have developed so far in political and economic life, or even that are aspired to in contractarian prescriptions. (Held 122)

We need a model that allows for organic connections, some more fundamental than others, among people, connections of dependency and interdependency of many kinds. (Wolgast 147)

The model of interpersonal relationships preferred by feminists to that of liberalism is not unitary, but "acknowledges many kinds of relations among people, and many kinds of social roles, and other kinds of interest than self-interest. . . . competition will be only one of the relations among people where determinations of justice apply." A model such as this acknowledges the diversity of human beings and human relationships, and that alone accords it superiority over liberalism's, which, as we have seen, especially ignores traditional women, children, and the relationships in which they are involved. Women will "fit in [this new model] in a variety of ways and roles" (Wolgast 156–57) because relationships between males will not be taken as the norm at the outset, because the complexity of human connections will not be reduced to a unitary ideal, and because it will be assumed that as sexism has differentiated the lives of the sexes, women have lessons to teach about relationships.

One of the questions with which feminist political theory concerns itself is how to resolve the tension, most felt by women, between care for and obligations to others and care for and obligations to one's self. It is necessary to "envision a society that grants each of us our 'individual dignity' but does not allow us to lose sight of our connections to each other."[17] Women's roles have frequently meant obliteration and sacrifice of the self, or redefinition of one's self and self-interest predominantly in terms of and in relations to others. The communitarian solution to liberalism's impoverished social life fails, however, to solve or even seriously address this enforced self-abnegation. Because communitarians see the social problem as fragmentation, their answer is connection. They favor tradition and applaud mores because they offer place, security, coherence, and stability. But the problem for women has not been solitude and lack of commitment, and the feminist alternative is neither simply connection nor simply separation. A feminist vision also necessarily entails critical reevaluation and restructuring of such engendered institutions and practices as the family, the sexual division of labor, and the connections between private and public. Contemporary communitarians do not see sexual differentiation as particularly problematic; in fact, it is often held up as a cure to *other* (read: important) social ills. At that point feminists and communitarians truly part ways.

Political Community

Understanding Liberalism

Communitarianism

For liberal individualism a community is simply an arena in which individuals each pursue their own self-chosen conception of the good life, and political institutions exist to provide that degree of order which makes such self-determined activity

Feminism

[L]iberal philosophers seek to develop a political theory that is independent of any substantive claims about the nature of the good life or of human happiness or fulfillment. Individuals are entitled to set their own ends. . . . They see the state as the neu-

possible. Government and law are, or ought to be, neutral between rival conceptions of the good life for man, and hence, although it is the task of government to promote law-abiding-ness, it is in the liberal view no part of the legitimate function of government to inculcate any one moral outlook. (MacIntyre 182)

tral arbiter of conflicting social interests, whose task is to protect individual rights and so to defend against the tyranny of any individual or group. (Jaggar 174, 200)

What liberalism professes to offer, according to communitarians and feminists, is a limited, neutral state that provides the conditions of "liberty" and "protection" in which individuals can pursue their private interests and goods as they define them. MacIntyre agrees with Ronald Dworkin that "the central doctrine of modern liberalism is the thesis that questions about the *good life for man* or the ends of human life are to be regarded from the public standpoint as systematically unsettlable. . . . The rules of morality and law hence are not to be derived from or justified in terms of some more fundamental conception of the good for man" (MacIntyre 112; emphasis in original). This is also Sandel's conceptualization of "deontological liberalism": "society, being composed of a plurality of persons, each with his own aims, interests, and conceptions of the good, is best arranged when it is governed by principles that do not *themselves* presuppose any particular conception of the good" (Sandel I: emphasis in original). Individuals have rights, and equal rights at that, and the task of the liberal state is to preserve them. It does this by protecting individuals from one another, and by itself not interfering with what is properly an individual's private concern.

This political posture follows, as does the liberal view of social relations, from liberalism's atomism: separate, self-interested individuals demand a politics that imposes no ends but enables the fulfillment of the individual's independently chosen ones. "The standard liberal argument for neutrality is an induction from social fragmentation. Since dissociated individuals will never agree on the good life, the state must allow them to live as they think best, subject only to John Stuart Mill's harm principle, without endorsing or sponsoring any particular understanding of what 'best' means" (Walzer 16).

Just as there is considerable agreement between feminist and communitarian understandings of liberalism's perspectives on the self and on social relations, so is there considerable agreement between them concerning liberalism's concept of political community. Perhaps most importantly, both note that liberalism accepts a politics of conflict that leads to the need for government as mediator. There are, however, some differences in emphasis among the portrayals of liberalism that will become significant. The aspect of liberal politics that gets most attention from feminists is the gap between neutrality in theory and partiality in practice, itself related to the larger problem of liberalism's public-private distinction and the role of government in each. The aspect of the liberal state that gets most attention from communitarians is government's misguided role as a neutral "referee" of values.

Critiques of Liberalism

Communitarianism

Liberal democracy may not be a theory of political community at all. It does not so much provide a justification for politics as it offers a politics that justifies individual rights. It is concerned more to promote individual liberty than to secure public justice, to advance interests rather than to discover goods, and to keep men safely apart rather than to bring them fruitfully together. As a consequence, it is capable of fiercely resisting every assault on the individual—his privacy, his property, his interests, and his rights—but is far less effective in resisting assaults on community or justice or citizenship or participation. (Barber 4)

Feminism

Liberal theory does not provide the language or concepts to help us understand the various kinds of human interdependence which are part of the life of both families and polities, nor to articulate a feminist vision of "the good life."[18]

[R]ights oversimplify complex power relations . . . [T]he resort to rights can be effectively countered by the resort to competing rights . . . [R]ights formulated to protect the individual against the state, or the weak against the strong, may be appropriated by the more powerful.[19]

[T]he liberal notion of "the private" has included what has been called "woman's sphere" as "male property" and sought not only to preserve it from the interference of the public realm but also to keep those who "belong" in that realm—women—from the life of the public. (Dietz 4)

For communitarians, the liberal political world, in which all that people share is protection from one another by an impartial state, leaves people without a common moral anchor, requires of them morally nothing higher than law-abidingness, and abdicates its responsibility for moral education. "Liberalism teaches respect for the distance of self and ends. . . . By putting the self beyond the reach of politics, it makes human agency an article of faith rather than an object of continuing attention and concern, a premise of politics rather than its precarious achievement. This misses the pathos of politics and also its most inspiring possibilities" (Sandel 183). According to communitarians, liberal politics follows from and reinforces atomistic individualism. The successes of the liberal state concern only its ability to protect the self-interested and isolated self, via structures and practices such as property rights, privacy claims, and interest-group politics. Social skills and feelings are not consciously cultivated, deeply restricting the style and substance of political life.

While communitarians find liberalism's politics inadequate, feminists find it at times mythical and at times positively injurious to women. More fully, communitarians speak as if liberalism were basically good at doing what it set out to do, but argue that it does not set out to do the right things. While feminists, too, question whether liberal principles can or should be the ones guiding the state, they also challenge liberalism for its failure in practice to do for both sexes what in principle it sets out to do.

Feminists evaluate liberalism's politics from a vantage point that reveals dynamics not attended to by communitarians. Catherine MacKinnon discusses how "liberal neutrality" in fact amounts to "substantive misogyny."[20] In the face of existing sexual inequality, a politics that, in the name of neutrality, refuses to take sides is in reality taking sides with the more powerful, men, allowing them to maintain their dominance through state policy of noninterference. Feminist critiques of liberal politics challenge its pretense to (gender) neutrality in a second way: feminists wonder how a state can be considered neutral that has upheld sexual segregation in employment, continues in public policy to prefer the nuclear heterosexual family over all other familial arrangements, considers affirmative action reverse discrimination, and refuses, on "privacy" grounds, to "interfere" in cases of domestic abuse, even while it outlaws "private" sexual acts between consenting adult members of the same sex.

Further, granting "rights" to the less powerful, a time-honored liberal solution, receives mixed reviews from feminists. True, gaining rights is a victory over those who would prefer little restraint on the potential exploitation of women.[21] But problems remain: private (male) power is often untouched by and impervious to (women's) formal rights; social and economic factors can limit the exercise of women's rights; and appeals to rights tend to treat the sexes (and individuals generally) as adversaries, thus reinforcing a problematical politics.

As Marxist feminists might prefer, liberal rights are fictitious coverups veiling the class rule of men. "Marxist feminists would have us recognize that a system of economics and gender rooted in capitalist, male-dominated structures underlies much of liberal ideology, from the notion of independent rational man to the conception of separate private and public realms, from the value of individualism to the equation of freedom with free trade" (Dietz 8). In fact, many feminists present a view of the liberal state as male-dominated, a concept parallel to the Marxist notion of a class-dominated state. One understanding of the destructiveness of the patriarchal liberal state, not subscribed to only by Marxist feminists, is offered by Hartsock:

> The masculine gender carried by power intensifies the tensions of community and leads to the construction of an even more conflictual and false community than that formed by means of exchange. It is a community both in theory and in fact obsessed with revenge and structured by conquest and domination. . . . These dynamics of conquest and domination mean that the gain of one participant can come only at the expense of the other's submission, humiliation, or even death.[22]

Because it is infused with patriarchal principles and processes, feminists would necessarily insist not on a state that reasserts *its* rights in the moral domain, as communitarians desire, but one that reassesses its own ethics.

Feminists and communitarians share a deep concern about the social and political consequences of a polity based on individual advantage. Many communitarians see the rise of self-interest as causally connected to the fall of a common moral sense in political communities and thus look to a resurrection of the latter as a solution to the problems of liberal politics. Feminists see the consequences of the liberal state as significantly different for the two sexes and urge attention to women's communities and networks for both insight into liberalism and ideas for alternatives to self-interested individualism. Here it becomes clear how criticisms of liberalism that are "gender-blind" are also "gender-biased"; the problems of liberalism most specific to women are ignored in the gender-blind critiques, and the call for a return to "a common moral vision" or, more common today, to "traditional values," is a gender-biased solution that does not speak from or to the lives of many women.

Alternatives to the Liberal View

Communitarianism

The application of that measure [of goodness] in a community whose shared aim is the realization of the human good presupposes . . . a wide range of agreement in that community on goods and virtues, and it is this agreement which makes possible the kind of bond between citizens which, on Aristotle's view, constitutes a *polis*. That bond is the bond of friendship. . . . Indeed from an Aristotelian point of view a modern liberal political society can appear only as a collection of citizens of nowhere who have banded together for their common protection. They possess at best that inferior form of friendship which is founded on mutual advantage. . . . They have abandoned the moral unity of Aristotelianism. (MacIntyre 146)

Feminism

A valuable alternative conception of politics . . . is perhaps best called the democratic one, and it takes politics to be the collective and participatory engagement of citizens in the determination of the affairs of their community. The community may be the neighborhood, the city, the state, the region, or the nation itself. What counts is that all matters relating to the community are undertaken as "the people's affairs." (Dietz 14)

[T]he conception of power as dominance is partial and misleading . . . one must not take the question of who rules whom to be the most critical political issue. (Hartsock 224)

There are so many visions of political community that perhaps it is impossible to represent them fairly here. Communitarian schemes range from MacIntyre's conventionalist Aristotelianism and Sandel's revitalized civic republicanism to Barber's Rousseauean participatory democracy. Feminist visions run the gamut from Sara Ruddick's maternal politics to Marge Piercy's small-town, ecologically minded democracies and Alison Jaggar's socialist feminist state. There is overlap as well as diversity among these theorists, most obvious in their frequent advocacy of democratic and socialist communities. Too often, however, the overlap is merely nominal. Focusing only on the common ground of democracy or socialism may conceal the different and often incompatible sets of political concerns and arrangements behind feminist and communitarian versions of each. One illustration of how feminists and communitarians diverge in their visions of community is the striking contrast in their attitudes toward ancient Greece.

MacIntyre's *After Virtue* devotes three chapters exclusively to ancient Greece. It is fair to say that his picture of community is very strongly and positively affected by the ancient Greek polities, even if he does not accept them as flawless. (There is, however, precious little evidence of his finding fault with them.)

These "heroic societies," as MacIntyre calls them, are marked by certain "key features": "Every individual has a given role and status within a well-defined and highly determinate system of roles and statuses. . . . [T]here is for each status a prescribed set of duties and privileges. There is also a clear understanding of what actions are required to perform these and what actions fall short" (MacIntyre 115).

As Okin notes, "one is left with the impression that it is [MacIntyre's] conscious intention to make the reader forget about the exclusionary nature of Aristotle's views about who could lead 'the good life for a human being,' " or who was capable of Aristotle's highest form of friendship. "[H]is benign interpretation de-emphasizes both the social hierarchy of heroic societies and the heavy sanctions that reinforced it."[23] Once again, then, the gloss painted on a picture of hierarchy, exclusion, and degradation by MacIntyre comes at precisely those points where feminists would scour the surface and reveal all the undercoats. In this case the difference is so striking that feminists seem quite justified in their lack of enthusiasm for communitarianism.

> [T]he Greek understanding of politics and power rested more directly and explicitly than ours on the division between women and men, between the household, a private and apolitical space, and the *polis*, a public and political space. This division was, moreover, a division between a realm of necessity and a realm of freedom, a realm held to be characterized by inequality and a realm seen as populated by equals, a realm described as dominated by the body and a realm where the soul or intellect was held to be dominant. All of this both rested on and reinforced a profound misogyny. (Hartsock 187)

Feminists should be wary of communitarian calls for moral unity. Such calls may signal a readiness to accept grave social inequalities and an insensitivity to the enriching power of differences.

Conclusion

The writers explored here all prefer a more communal theory and practice than is found in liberalism. A final, more subterranean, issue helps explain the distance between feminist and communitarian thought: their motives for rejecting liberalism.

MacIntyre's *After Virtue* is informed by the "grave disorder" of moral anomie, which "perhaps . . . a very few—recognised as a catastrophe" (MacIntyre 2, 3). The concerns at the center of his enterprise seem most directly to involve and be felt by moral theorists—truly a "very few." The "castrophe" is that there is "no rational way of securing moral agreement in our culture" (MacIntyre 6). That we are experiencing a moral decline is shown by our "complacency" with "moral pluralism," when what we really have is "an unharmonious melange of ill-assorted fragments" of viewpoints (MacIntrye 10). Given the cultural power of "emotivism," we are quite comfortable with the view that "all moral judgments are *nothing but* expressions of preference, expressions of attitude or feelings," despite the fact that this "Weberian vision of the world cannot be rationally sustained" (MacIntyre 19, 11, 103; emphasis in original). MacIntyre's concern is with "modern moral theorists" who are faced with "insoluble problems . . . [by] modern moral utterance and practice" (MacIntyre 104–5), who are searching for "impersonal . . . standards of justice or generosity or duty" (MacIntyre 9). It is not clear that MacIntyre's problem is necessarily so remote from the political concerns that inform feminism, but the inference from his writing is that feminist issues are not necessarily relevant to a search for justice or virtue. Immoral misogynist behavior must, again, take a back seat, this time to moral agreement in theory. It is then unsurprising that his "vindication" of Aristotelean ethics and politics and the "way of life" they entail (MacIntyre 111) seem so politically uncritical from a feminist perspective.

Much of the same can be said of Michael Sandel's *Liberalism and the Limits of Justice*. He tells us at the outset that the limits of (liberal) justice he argues for "are not practical but conceptual" (Sandel 1). His enterprise of showing the incoherence of a "concept of a subject given prior to and independent of its objects" has as its end the refutation of the liberal "claim for the primacy of justice" (Sandel 7). Feminists are not necessarily unconcerned about the rhetorical consistency of liberalism or whether the right is prior to the good. But, unlike Sandel, feminists find the limits of liberal justice most dramatically visible in the "practical" world; little would be gained, from a feminist perspective, if liberalism were made more tidy conceptually and left as dirty in practice.

Finally, the authors of *Habits of the Heart* speak thus of the "tensions" analyzed in their text: "We strongly assert the value of our self-reliance and autonomy. We deeply feel the emptiness of a life without sustaining social commitments. Yet we are hesitant to articulate our sense that we need one another as much as we need to stand alone, for fear that if we did we would lose our independence altogether" (Bellah et al. 151). The standpoint from which this passage is written is that of the traditional male, endless usages of "we" and "our" notwithstanding. This is the male who is more comfortable asserting his autonomy than acknowledging his need for or debt to others, most fearful of all of losing what he calls his independence. Traditional woman's starting point is the opposite:

she is more comfortable acknowledging her need for others than asserting her autonomy, most fearful of losing her connections to others. Indeed, the individual stories in *Habits of the Heart* show this to be true, and still the point is missed. The authors continue to treat the male experience as the norm, rendering women's experiences invisible, outside the mainstream of supposedly universal human experience. That which could be learned from women's unique experiences with community, positive and negative, is lost.

It is astonishing that in the long lists of modern woes cited by communitarians one almost never finds items such as the feminization of illiteracy and poverty (by the year 2000 virtually all "officially" poor people in the United States will be women or children), rape (perpetrated on perhaps one of every four women, compromising the freedom of all women), domestic violence (half of all married women can expect at least one violent episode at the hands of their mate), pornography (an $8 billion a year industry in the United States alone), reproductive issues from compulsory motherhood to forced sterilization, inadequate and unaffordable child care, prostitution, child abuse, sexual harassment, or undervaluing of women's labor. If any one of these is mentioned, it is too often as a mere symptom of a "real" or "bigger" problem that has nothing to do with male domination.

Given the sexism, racism, and homophobia pervasive in most cultures, educational systems, workplaces, and political practices, unless people start out explicitly committed *not* to discriminate, they usually end up discriminating. This understanding of how oppression is maintained is, of course, the basis of affirmative action policies. Communitarianism lacks feminist consciousness and commitment to resolving problems of gender hierarchy. Thus, it usually ignores and therefore perpetuates those problems: it ends up with a white male vision, as "unintentional" and as thorough as that found anywhere. Feminists do indeed find a "perilous ally" (Friedman 277) in communitarianism, whether it is Plato's, Rousseau's, or MacIntyre's, and will continue to as long as communitarianism is isolationist in its politics.

We are in the midst of what Michael Walzer calls "a recurrent [communitarian] critique" of liberalism (Walzer 6). The disciplines at least of philosophy and political theory are awash in communitarian attacks upon liberals and responding defenses of liberalism. Walzer sees such debate as useful even if, likely, never-ending. A constant feature of the recurring debate that Walzer neglects to note, however, is the absence of concern by both sides about sexual equality. To the extent that the communitarian-liberal debate continues to command so much attention from social and political theorists, feminism continues to be relatively ignored. Antifeminism and communitarianism have a "tradition" of coexistence and cooperation, and we learn more about both by studying them together. Because patriarchal values and institutions continue to pervade communitarian visions, feminists most definitely must persist in developing full-fledged communitarian visions of our own.

Notes

Reprinted from *Gendered Community: Rousseau, Sex, and Politics* (New York: New York University Press, 1993): 121–48 and 172–4, by permission of the author and the publisher.

1. The best text on this is probably Zillah Eisenstein's *The Radical Future of Liberal Feminism* (New York: Longman, 1981).

2. Christopher Lasch, "The Communitarian Critics of Liberalism," in *Community in America: The Challenge of Habits of the Heart*, edited by Charles Reynolds and Ralph Norman (Berkeley: University of California Press, 1988), 175.

3. Alasdair MacIntyre, *After Virtue: A Study in Moral Theory* (Notre Dame, Ind.: University of Notre Dame Press, 1981), 232–33.

4. Benjamin Barber, *Strong Democracy: Participatory Politics for a New Age* (Berkeley: University of California Press, 1984), 33.

5. Marilyn Friedman, "Feminism and Modern Friendship: Dislocating the Community," *Ethics* 99 (January 1989): 275.

6. Mary Dietz, "Context Is All: Feminism and Theories of Citizenship," *Daedalus* 116 (Fall 1987): 5.

7. Alison Jaggar, *Feminist Politics and Human Nature* (Totowa, N.J.: Rowman & Allanheld, 1983), 42.

8. Not everyone agrees that these features of the self are necessarily part of liberalism. There is a significant effort to counter the charges against liberalism made by communitarians, in particular. See, for example, Michael Walzer, "The Communitarian Critique of Liberalism," *Politi-*

cal Theory 18 (February 1990): 173–84; Will Kymlicka, "Liberalism and Communitarianism," *Canadian Journal of Philosophy* 18 (June 1988): 181–95; and Allen Buchanan, "Assessing the Communitarian Critique of Liberalism," *Ethics* 99 (July 1989). Also see Susan Wendell," A (Qualified) Defense of Liberal Feminism," *Hypatia: A Journal of Feminist Philosophy* 2 (Summer 1987): 65–94.

9. Chantal Mouffe, "American Liberalism and Its Critics: Rawls, Taylor, Sandel and Walzer," *Praxis International* 8 (July 1988): 198.

10. Seyla Benhabib and Drucilla Cornell, "Introduction: Beyond the Politics of Gender," *Feminism as Critique*, ed. Seyla Benhabib and Drucilla Cornell (Minneapolis: University of Minnesota Press, 1987), 12.

11. Michael J. Sandel, *Liberalism and the Limits of Justice* (Cambridge: Cambridge University Press, 1982), 179.

12. Good examples of this include Naomi Scheman, "Individualism and the Objects of Psychology," in *Discovering Reality: Feminist Perspectives on Epistemology, Metaphysics, Methodology and the Philosophy of Science*, ed. S. Harding and M. Hintikka (Dordrecht: Reidel, 19873); Sara Ruddick, "Maternal Thinking," *Feminist Studies* 6 (Summer 1980): 342–67; and Nancy Holmstrom, "Do Women Have a Distinct Nature?" in *Women and Values: Readings in Recent Feminist Philosophy*, ed. Marilyn Pearsall (Belmont, Calif.: Wadsworth, 1986), 15.

13. Robert Bellah, Richard Madsen, William Sullivan, Ann Swidler, and Steven Tipton, *Habits of the Heart: Individualism and Commitment in American Life* (Berkeley: University of California Press, 1985), 107.

14. Virginia Held, "Non-Contractual Society: A Feminist View," *Canadian Journal of Philosophy Suppl.* 13 (1987): 124–25.

15. Elizabeth Wolgast, *Equality and the Rights of Women* (Ithaca, N.Y.: Cornell University Press, 1980), 154.

16. Jane Mansbridge, *Beyond Self-Interest* (Chicago: University of Chicago Press, 1990), ix.

17. M. Elizabeth Albert, "In the Interest of the Public Good? New Questions for Feminism," in *Community in America: The Challenge of Habits of the Heart*, ed. Charles H. Reynolds and Ralph V. Norman (Berkeley: University of California Press, 1988), 88.

18. Mary Lyndon Shanley, "Marital Slavery and Friendship," *Political Theory* 8 (May 1980): 360.

19. Carol Smart, *Feminism and the Power of the Law* (New York: Routledge, 1989), 144–45.

20. Catherine MacKinnon, *Feminism Unmodified: Discourses on Life and Law* (Cambridge, MA: Harvard University Press, 1987), 15.

21. Patricia Williams, *The Alchemy of Race and Rights* (Cambridge, MA: Harvard University Press, 1991).

22. Nancy Hartsock, *Money, Sex and Power: Toward a Feminist Historical Materialism* (Boston: Northeastern University Press, 1983), 177.

23. Susan Moller Okin, *Justice, Gender, and the Family* (New York: Basic Books, 1989), 45, 49.

Reversals as a Way of Seeing

This is an essay on political strategy. How do we open eyes and ears, how do we get defenses down enough for feminism to be part of a conversation rather than written off at the outset? In teaching I have used a wonderful novel, Gerd Brantenberg's Egalia's Daughters: A Satire of the Sexes. *Although the book is a satire rather than a reversal, it is the reversals within it that my students report as most eye-opening and as catching them so off guard that they saw and heard things they wouldn't have seen and heard as easily or as well another way. The ability of reversals to open a dialogue seemed worth exploring in my academic field of political theory.*

The most important single principle of learning, we now understand, is that you must find ways to connect new concepts, new ideas to the ideas that are already in the heads of youngsters. Teaching is bridge building. That's why when you walk into a classroom of a fine teacher, I contend that the word you will hear most often when a teacher is explaining something is the word "like." Like. The teacher is always saying, well it's like this, it's like that, helping students make connections.

Lee Shulman, "The Bridges Teachers Build"

8

🌿 🌿 🌿

Reversals as a Way of Seeing

Part I

Step for a few minutes into a world where everything changes when one thing changes—a world in which women dominate men. For simplicity's sake, let's look only at one subfield of one academic discipline in this topsy-turvy world: political theory. The history of political theory is peopled entirely by women: Aristonia and Platonia in antiquity, Saints Thomasina and Augustinia in medieval times, and Nicole MacVillain, Jan Block, Donna Bobs, Jean-Jackie Trousseau, Jane Stuart Miller and Carla Marcus in modernity. Even the more minor figures, such as Jeanette Bodine and Roberta Fillmore, are women.

Looking at college curricula and theory textbooks, those few who notice such things wonder why there have never been any great male theorists, and they guess that this reflects on the general superiority of the female intellect. Certainly they have heard that uttered often enough, called upon as an explanation for everything from women's higher scores on standardized tests, to men's underrepresentation among Nobel Prize winners. But one day some men have the opportunity to get together and begin asking questions that later culminate in a thorough reappraisal of the history of political theory.

They studied the great political tradition together, with their gaze focused on what was said about gender, the grounds on which it was defended, and its ramifications. This itself was no small task, given how trained they were to glide over such problems in favor of ones supposedly more central. They had to stop occasionally and wonder how it was that scholars found the treatment of men—of half the human species—a trivial aside, irrelevant to understanding or evaluating someone's political thought. Yet ink was generously spent over such problems as the distinctions between the early and late Carla Marcus and the similarity between Jean-Jackie Trousseau and her character the Savvy Victor in her text *Emily*.

Sensitive to every nuance, as men are trained to be, their work confirmed that one can find amazing things when one opens one's eyes. With constantly renewed astonishment, they found in text after text that women were the real subjects of political theory and activity. Men were looked at last: their inferiority was defined by their difference from the female norm, their nature was described in terms of the tasks women, or the culture women created, needed them to perform, and control over them was justified by the threat they posed to this matriarchal world order. Perhaps most common of all, men were said to lack whatever quality a given philosopher supposed made people complete, unique, divine, or happy. To be male and to be human were portrayed as mutually exclusive, and what being male boiled down to was serving women and children. Until they got together they had each wondered privately if men were the problem or if political theory was the problem.

They found that each of them had tried to read the texts as if men were included. First they tried supposing that the degrading characterizations and stereotypes referred to *other* men. This effort was fruitless at best, self-defeating at worst. The words seemed as untrue of other men as of themselves. Gender identification made it tough to imagine oneself in the place of another so clearly marked as of the opposite sex. (Passages about how the fully human person should treat her husband always got in the way, too.) And, as they later realized, this strategy perpetuated division among men and allowed derogatory, antimale sentiments to go unchallenged. Besides, thinking of oneself as an exception only goes so far when you're virtually the only one looking at yourself that way.

They had also tried just translating "women" into "people" as they read but soon discovered that the authors' sexism was not simply a matter of semantics, not some detachable appendage, but an intrinsic part of the whole work. You couldn't just "add men and mix," as they later expressed it. How, for example, could they imagine that Aristonia had women *and* men in mind as citizens, when the leisure women had to dedicate to the polis was a direct result of the domestic enslavement of men? How could they assume that an endorsement of representative government for women meant or could mean representation of and by men, when women were the subjects and actors in politics by virtue of being heads of household, representatives and beneficent mistresses of their husbands and children?

Not everything they found was so depressing. One of their most rewarding and remarkable discoveries was that there *were* great male philosophers. Their discoveries of lost figures and lost ideas were accompanied by tremendous intellectual and emotional excitement, a powerful combination that one sex seems so eager to dismiss. They realized how much they themselves had come to believe in male inferiority when they discovered their joy and surprise at finding that, despite all the forces conspiring to keep men uneducated and domesticated throughout history, men did write political theory: profound, playful, passionate theory. Interestingly, like the few women who wrote in support of sexual equality, the works of these men remained unpublished. Or, if published, they remained out of print. Or, if in print, were untranslated. Or, if translated, remained unstudied. Or, if studied, were not written about, for graduate students don't get jobs and professors don't get published researching what are widely considered minor figures and marginal topics.

Think how exciting it was when they realized that Walter Stonecraft, despite his virtual invisibility in standard histories of political theory, wrote a treatise at least as innovative and as representative of early liberal philosophy as those by Jan Block or Jane Stuart Miller. And Simon de Rover accomplished similar things in existential philosophy. That taught them something about the extent to which some would go to allow women and only women to define the parameters and subjects of a theory. Think how empowering it was when the now self-proclaimed masculists challenged the commonly accepted notion that Jane Stuart Miller only wrote *On the Subjection of Men* because of the undue and unnatural influence of her overbearing and somewhat testerical husband Harry Taylor Miller. It helped them see that even if you are female, utterly sincere, and well respected, you cannot write that men are equal without being ignored, being ridiculed, and having your womanhood questioned. That taught them something about the intensity of the forces working to keep men subordinant and about the intensity with which they would have to work to liberate men. And they must certainly have tingled with nervous excitement over the fact that even in those dark Middle Ages men spoke out in defense of their sex, as Chris de Zan did in *The Book of the City of Gentlemen*. Such figures existed, and they were part of the great history not only of political theory but of resistance to sexism.

As they continued to read together and to analyze the forces behind the disappearance of these voices, the masculists became increasingly convinced that the gender problem in political thought was due to matriarchy, its disdain for anything associated with the male, including men themselves, and its willingness to sacrifice the male for the interests of women. The shameful treatment of men in the history of theory was only finally comprehensible as one of many manifestations of female domination. Things clicked, aided by similar discoveries both inside and outside the ivory tower. Masculists were at work everywhere analyzing, deconstructing, and re-visioning what had once seemed obvious and uncontroversial. It was easy, for example, to link the bias in political theory to the bias in public policy, for in both the norm defining problems and constructing remedies is a female one. Similarly, the trivialization of men by philosophers resembled the fate of the gender gap in American politics, for in both men become a mere puzzle for strategists to solve or manage for female advantage. When they reached this masculist understanding, *it* seemed so uncontroversial and obvious they couldn't remember how it had ever been anything else.

It felt the way it feels when you first get glasses after years of squinting or, better, the way it feels when you finally and suddenly solve a complex mystery story despite the author's numerous attempts to confuse and mislead you throughout. "Of course," you say. "I should have seen that."

These men had dutifully studied row upon row of works regarded—by those women said to know them best—as the most insightful, truthful, and impartial. Yet at the end, with a boldness often thought to be reserved for women, they challenged the motives, truth, and objectivity of virtually every woman in the history of theory, as well as the women who interpreted them and the women who regarded the academic inclusion of works by men as sacrilege, a distortion of "our" cultural heritage.

When they asked who was included in the "our" whose cultural heritage we are to cherish and preserve, these men's libbers declared that because of sexism every culture actually includes two cultures, one female and one male. They went so far as to assert that men's was as rich, complete, inspiring, and worthy of study and emulation as was women's. Some—though, we are assured, only a radical and strident minority—even considered men's heritage to be superior. The masculists talked of finding in political theory written by men: less concern with glory and exclusion, less tolerance of abuse and violence, and attention not only to what divides people but also to what connects them. They claimed that men have been less corrupted by power and less trained in dominance and conquest than women have been, though I can only guess at some of what they mean, and that this difference has led to understandings of the self and of personal and social relationships fed by less greed and more compassion, less jealousy and more trust.

Well, it *is* true that Platonia makes the rather damning assertion that in every occupation the female is superior to the male. I have double-checked, and it is also clear that Aristonia said of men that their rationality was incomplete, and thus they should serve their female superiors. Even those we call saints, yes, these too are guilty. Perhaps you, like me, hadn't noticed that Saint Thomasina felt it necessary to ask in the *Sumo* "Whether the Men Should Have Been

Made in the First Production of Things." I'm not sure I grasp their point entirely, but I've heard the men's libbers say that Nicole Mac-Villain should be criticized for seeing in men that which women should fear and conquer. Jan Block they read as still living in the state of nature. Donna Bobs, for all they care, could be the next victim of the war of all against all, for she ignored the more cooperative history of men in claiming aggressiveness is just part of human nature. Jean-Jackie Trousseau—well, what do *you* think should be the fate of the supposedly great democrat who says man is born to serve and please woman?

Part II

That's some of what gender bias in political theory looks like, in reverse. In the hands of male chauvinists and certain comedians, gender reversal is a tactic used to undermine feminism by making it look ridiculous, almost sacrilegious. In the hands of feminists, however, gender reversal is used to help us see the invisible, the unconscious. When we're asked our reaction to a woman saying, "No husband of mine is going to work!" we come to see how ordinary yet unnoted expressions of male control over women are. When someone suggests that if men got pregnant all methods of birth control would be 100 percent effective, we come to see how powerfully but invisibly sexism influences policy and research agendas. When someone suggests that theorizing done by women that reduces man to women's inferior and servant might be something less than perfectly objective, it helps us to see the extent to which we have unjustifiably yet unquestioningly accepted the decrees of political theorists both about their impartiality and about women's marginality.

Gender bias, like most other kinds of discrimination, comes in a range of forms. Too often we recognize as sexist only the most overt statements and actions limiting and stigmatizing women as women, as members of a group that is itself caricatured, misrepresented, and maligned.

One of the more blatant forms of gender bias is that which reserves all of the traits, jobs, ambitions, and roles considered good for men and assigns and attributes that which is deemed secondary and inferior to the nature and province of women. In Aristotle women have deficient rationality, live in a permanent position of being ruled, and do not participate in public deliberations. Left to men are the most revered capacities—to reason, to rule, and to govern—and the most highly esteemed and powerful positions in which to develop and exercise them. In Freud women lack a penis and have deficient moral reasoning. It is left to men like himself, uninfluenced by womb envy, to reach the heights of moral development. If being created directly by God is the source of human dignity, then women's secondary biblical creation is the source of her inferiority and subordination. If being able to rise above the bodily, the sensual, and the physical is what grants one entrance into the fully human, then women's capacity to bear children excludes her as bound to an inferior realm. With minor varieties on a theme, and despite their contradictions with each other, male political philosophers reissue such self-righteous edicts century after century. Actually, I think the inability to agree on what essentially differentiates women and men, and with what consequences, arises because it's a secondary issue. What really matters is keeping the sexes polarized and hierarchicalized, and whatever arguments work best in a given historical era and philosophical framework will be employed. That is, women's ambitions, capacities, desires, and interests are not really the subject of independent, rigorous, and sincere inquiry but are an afterthought, described in terms of whatever complements the male subject.

In a related form of gender bias, theories not only ascribe to women a secondary and inferior nature and function but present women as a serious threat to men, a threat men rightly attempt to conquer. One of women's roles in Augustine is as temptress, an aspect of the devil's evil designs. Nietzsche's overman creates values and battles conventionality; his woman is but a "dangerous plaything." The connection between women's threat and violence against women could not be clearer than in Nietzsche, for, in *Thus Spake Zarathustra*, after describing woman as dangerous, a plaything, base in her soul, and superficial, he writes, "Do you go to women? Do not forget the whip!" Thus spake misogyny.

Disdain for women in the history of theory also takes the form of silence. This is a somewhat less obvious form of bias. Just as whites too often don't notice the absence of people of color at certain gatherings, and as the able-bodied rarely note the absence of ramps, until feminism entered the academy few seemed to notice or attribute significance to another form of bias: silence, the absence of women in the philosophies that are supposed to help us to understand ourselves and our relations with each other. Plato's *Republic* is an example of women's absence in philosophical dialogue and its consequences, as another essay in this collection explores (see chapter 4). Exclusion can speak loud and clear. It leaves us a tradition in which what certain men have valued is institutionalized and justified, whether that be military valor, as in Homeric times, or acquisitive victory in the marketplace, as it was for several of the moderns.

And the model of the ideal, good, or common person is similarly biased. Liberalism, for example, conceives of the self as an atomistic individual, rationally maximizing her or his self-interest. Marxism looks at capitalism and sees the worker as exploited and alienated through wage slavery. Neither liberalism nor Marxism include, for example, the unpaid mother, sometimes rationally, sometimes not so rationally, contributing to the well-being of others.

A last form of bias is a bias against feminist theory itself. Before feminism, as some would have it, there was no one and nothing granting academic acceptability to particular methods, subjects, disciplines, styles, or results. Now feminism is trying to impose its own bias on everyone, threatening true discourse with its power to grant medals of political correctness, bullying objectivity into submission. I must say that sometimes I take comfort in this vision as I daydream revenge, but it is far from reality with respect to both what feminism is doing and the power that it possesses to do it. Before we take pity on the poor powerless but objective scientists being harassed by feminist censors, we should at least ask whether this isn't a red herring. The clamor over political correctness seems to me to be an attempt to derail feminism by portraying it as destructive of everything that is good and dear in the academy—an attempt that, if successful, will permit us to avoid grappling with the sexism, racism, and homophobia pervasive in our institutions and practices.

That feminist theory is "unscholarly" or "ideological" is an accusation that refuses to consider the possibility that patriarchy is a bias. Dale Spender offers one only slightly sarcastic explanation for academia's lack of interest in recognizing feminist theory:

> Am I, a woman of the limited, non-authoritative, emotional, deviant and wrong sex, unschooled in the art-and-science of philosophy, being so presumptuous as to fly in the face of centuries of established philosophical tradition and to suggest that there is a fundamental, philosophical question about the nature of human existence that my "superiors" have not addressed? If no such question has arisen in the philosophical circles of the masters, can I not see that it must not be important—that is, if it is indeed a *real* question and not just a product of my sense of grievance and embitteredness, because I happen to be born of the wrong sex?[1]

Feminist theory is sometimes said to be biased because it has already concluded that men oppress women, and wrongly do so, and thus the field lacks neutrality. This implies that with the lone exception of women's studies, and some of its relatives such as ethnic studies, professors hold no substantive positions or, if they do, keep them out of the classroom. Although it's not a requirement for tenure or promotion, one would hope that after years of study, most professors would have some substantive position on some of what they teach. And every discipline and every subfield within a discipline has foregone conclusions, not only in notions about what to study and how to study it but in norms of what a "balanced ecosystem" is, a "healthy body," and a "free election." Political theory is not just formal debate of artificial and hypothetical issues and situations. It has to address real problems—and women's oppression is one of them. Theory is filled with substantive moral and political positions, from relativism, Marxism, and pluralism, to communitarianism, liberalism, and realism. In every case, feminism included, theoretical skills are brought to bear on the relevant set of issues, arguments are made and weighed on various sides, refutations are considered, and conclusions are reached.

Even with the most traditional rendering of the tasks and methods of political theory, feminist theory has a legitimate place. Arguments about women's nature, role, and status are found throughout the history of philosophy, from Plato to Rawls. Further, it has always been part of political inquiry to ask questions about human nature, convention, legitimate authority, ideology, majority tyranny, civil disobedience, and citizen rights and duties. Even this most time-honored list of topics makes clear that gender *is* a legitimate object of political theorizing and an important source of information required for addressing such questions. We needn't totally reconceive the field to see that it has been biased in its choice of questions, subjects, and examples.

Lest this sound too much like the argument that Marxists and capitalists all put on their shoes the same way, let me point out one last difference. Having taught both feminist theory and traditional theory, I think some of what makes many skeptical about feminist theory being theory is that so many students come out of these courses committed to political change—the material has a deep impact, personally, politically, and intellectually. But why should we not consider this impact something about feminist theory that makes it particularly exemplary rather than unacademic? Why do we pledge allegiance to the idea that what happens in the classroom is "only academic"? We underestimate our contribution and potential, as women once did in describing themselves individually as "just a housewife."

Since I've breezed through what a reversed gender bias might look and feel like and a few of the forms gender bias can take, I'd like to close with some quick thoughts about what unbiased political theory might look like and inquire into. In the university, theory classes and theory journals would probably cover the figures we are used to finding there, but they would cover them differently, considering as relevant their words on gender and the impact this has on their theory in general, and considering them only as part of the conversation about political life. Filling out the picture would be political thinkers such as Sappho, Christine de Pizan, Mary Wollstonecraft, Simone de Beauvoir, Harriet Taylor, Emma Goldman, Frances Wright, Margaret Fuller, the Grimke sisters, Susan B. Anthony, Charlotte Perkins Gilman, Virginia Woolf, Mary Daly, Adrienne Rich, Marilyn French, Angela Davis, Catherine MacKinnon, and so on. It's remarkable, but there's a whole other intellectual history out there of which we have all been robbed. It's a history that makes the tradition we know seem to be what it really is—a part of the story. It's time we got a less distorted and more heterogeneous picture, for the costs of this omission are wide and deep. As Adrienne Rich puts it in her incomparable way:

> What does a woman need to know, to become a self-conscious, self-defining human being? Doesn't she need a knowledge of her own history; . . . of the creative genius of women of the past—the skills and crafts and techniques and visions possessed by women in other times and cultures, . . . doesn't she need an analysis of her condition, a knowledge of the women thinkers of the past who have reflected on it, a knowledge too of women's world-wide individual rebellions and organized movements against economic and social injustice . . . Without such education, women have lived and continue to live in ignorance of our collective context, vulnerable to the projections of men's fantasies about us as they appear in art, in literature, in the sciences, in the media, in the so-called humanistic studies. . . . [E]nforced ignorance has been a crucial key to our powerlessness.[2]

An unbiased political theory would know that the personal is political and the political is personal. That is, the range of questions considered to be part of the discipline would be expanded, and the information used to answer them would be wider ranging. What might we find, for example, if studies in balances of power scrutinized not only relations between different branches of government but also relations between the sexes? What else would we learn about how power is maintained, and at what costs, if we looked for insight at domestic violence? At child rearing? What practices would such queries force us to reconsider?

What changes would ensue if we treated the bearing and rearing of children as the socially necessary labor it is, essential to survival and well-being, instead of treating it as nonproductive, nonpolitical, private, natural? What would happen if we imagined that values and concepts like self-interested rationality, consent, and one person, one vote applied not only to what we call the public sphere but also to the family? Alternatively, what would the world look like if concepts like nurture, family, trust, common good, and accommodation were applied to politics?

The division of life into public and private has been a safeguard against totalitarianism, but it has also worked to women's disadvantage: failing to protect her against abuse, defining her out of politics, and leaving her domestic labor unpaid. What institutional safeguards can protect the freedom of *both* sexes?

As a student, I read (or tried to read) political theory as if these great thinkers were including me, or at least my kind. Seeing the history of justifications for women's limitation, victimization, and exclusion was extremely dismaying. I wondered why the historical conversation about gender was so impoverished, so monotonous, so unchallenged. Finally I found the taint from sexism so pervasive, infecting so much beyond sexual relations, that trying to rid theories of their sexism came to feel, in Mary Daly's words, like trying to rid the KKK of its racism.[3]

The feminist reappraisal of political theory has shown that the historical conversation about gender has in fact not been unchallenged. We've only been hearing half of it. There is in feminist theory a revisioning of the landscape: a profound change in the questions we must ask and the answers we can live with. The male bias in political theory truly is pervasive. Feminism provides us with an opportunity for such theory to be more than it has been: more comprehensive, open to more possibilities, and more concerned with justice for more people.

Notes

This essay was originally written for presentation as the keynote address at the Indiana Political Science Association meeting, April 26, 1991. The audience was wonderfully receptive. I especially remember some graduate students from Notre Dame who expressed amazement that "someone who wrote this got their Ph.D. at Notre Dame." Indeed.

1. Dale Spender, *Women of Ideas and What Men Have Done to Them* (Winchester, Mass: Pandora, Unwin Hyman, 1982), 7.

2. Adrienne Rich, "Commencement Address at Smith College, 1979," in Rich, *On Lies, Secrets and Silence* (New York: Norton, 1979).

3. Mary Daly, "The Qualitative Leap beyond Patriarchal Religion," *Quest* 1 (Spring 1975), 22.

Remembering the Lady

I assign the letters between Abigail and John Adams to my "Women and the Law" class as one historical example of the interplay between gendered thinking in the law, politics, personal life, and theory. One semester, quite without planning, I found myself returning from classes, calling the letters up on my computer, and writing to Abigail as a way of sorting out for myself some of what was going on in my class, in my life, in feminism.

The response that follows combines personal anecdotes, historical research, and theoretical argument as aspects of feminist concerns that both more and less span the centuries from Abigail to today. The conversations here are between Abigail and me and between the centuries of feminism, on the one hand, and between John and me and between feminism and antifeminism, on the other hand.

The manner in which the theorists and the works included in the "Western Tradition" of social and political thought are chosen has also been questioned: why do standard discussions ignore J. S. Mill's "The Subjection of Women"? Why is Paine's reply to Burke's polemic against the French revolution studied, but not Mary Wollstonecraft's earlier reply? Why have the early socialists, who were concerned with relations between the sexes and new modes of household organisation, been dismissed as "utopian"? Why, more generally, are none of the feminist theorists' writing from the seventeenth century onward discussed, when the most minor male figures are given their due?

Carole Pateman, "Introduction: The Theoretical
Subversiveness of Feminism"

9

❦ ❦ ❦

Remembering the Lady:
A Letter to Abilagil Adams

In 1776 John and Abigail Adams exchanged the following letters:

Abigail to John:
　　—and by the way in the new Code of Laws which I suppose it will be necessary for you to make I desire you would Remember the Ladies, and be more generous and favourable to them than your ancestors. Do not put such unlimited power into the hands of the Husbands. Remember all Men would be tyrants if they could. If perticular care and attention is not paid to the Laidies we are determined to foment a Rebelion, and will not hold ourselves bound by any Laws in which we have no voice, or Representation. That your Sex are Naturally Tyrannical is a Truth so thoroughly established as to admit of no dispute, but such of you as wish to be happy willingly give up the harsh title of Master for the more tender and endearing one of Friend. Why then, not put it out of the power of the vicious and the Lawless to use us with cruelty and indignity with impunity. Men of Sense in all Ages abhor those customs which treat us only as the vassals of your Sex. Regard us then as Being placed by providence under your protection and in immitation of the Supreem Being make use of that power only for our happiness.

John to Abigail:
　　As to your extraordinary Code of Laws, I cannot but laugh. We

have been told that our Struggle has loosened the bands of Government every where. That Children and Apprentices were disobedient—that schools and Colledges were grown turbulent—that Indians slighted their Guardians and Negroes grew insolent to their Masters. But your Letter was the first Intimation that another Tribe more numerous and powerfull than all the rest were grown discontented. This is rather too coarse a Compliment but you are so saucy, I wont blot it out. Depend upon it, We know better than to repeal our Masculine systems. Altho they are in full Force, you know they are little more than Theory. We dare not exert our Power in its full Latitude. We are obliged to go fair, and softely, and in Practice you know We are the subjects. We have only the Name of Masters, and rather than give up this, which would compleatly subject Us to the Despotism of the Peticoat, I hope General Washington, and all our brave Heroes would fight. I am sure every good Politician would plot, as long as he would against Despotism, Empire, Monarchy, Aristocracy, Oligarchy, or Ochlocracy.

Abigail to John:
    I can not say that I think you very generous to the Ladies, for whilst you are proclaiming peace and good will to Men, Emancipating all Nations, you insist upon retaining an absolute power over Wives. But you must remember that Arbitrary power is like most other things which are very hard, very liable to be broken—and notwithstanding all your wise Laws and Maxims we have it in our power not only to free ourselves but to subdue our Masters, and without violence throw both your natural and legal authority at our feet—"Charm by accepting, by submitting sway Yet have our Humour most when we obey."

I thought Abigail deserved a response quite different from that offered by John.

—and by the way in the new Code of Laws which I suppose it will be necessary for you to make. . . .

When I first read these words, I thought about how exciting it might have been to live at the time of the "American Revolution." Through my studies I saw a time when people cared and argued about what freedom and independence meant, when it was respectable to resist tyranny, and when ideas about the nature, limits, and possibilities of government power were openly debated. This seemed to me a sad contrast with today, when people asked to identify the contents of the Bill of Rights guess that it is the Communist Manifesto and when the idea that government owes anybody anything has lost respectability if not meaning altogether. I imagined without really thinking about it that the "American Founding" was just as exciting, just as filled with possibilities for women as individuals and as members of the political communities existing in the colonies as for men.

I know now that what various groups of men fight for often has nothing to do with improving women's conditions. The "revolutionaries" fought not for freedom for all but for the elimination of certain forms of power, not against all threats to individual liberty but against certain dangers they wanted contained. In fact, they often persuaded skeptics to join them by making clear that they were not asking for *all* kinds of freedom; not, for example, for the freedom of women in marriage, or for the elimination of slavery, or for preservation of native cultures. They proved the worthiness and "reasonableness" of their cause, that is, by denying the legitimacy of other, more "foreign" and suspect causes.

To be heard one must be considered "reasonable" enough to warrant listening to. Commonly, to be considered reasonable is to offer proof of "sameness" rather than "saneness"—evidence of some significant area or degree of agreement with the listener and, too often, with the political status quo. Defenders of U.S. autonomy were a privileged minority whose case gained credibility by ostentatious show of their agreement with other ideas and practices of the empowered, no matter how oppressive the latter. That women as women were largely irrelevant as subjects to the so-called revolution was not anomalous but part of a larger historical pattern.

I have fewer illusions now and know that in times of "revolution" one is often called on to fall into line rather than to ask additional questions and voice further demands. The presence of conflict, between bodies or ideas, closes rather than opens debate. The need to be (what is called) unified against an (supposed) enemy squelches ideas, in fact turns them into a threat. I watched in the Gulf War as those in the United States who questioned official positions quickly got branded unpatriotic and extremist. "Rally

'round the flag!" challengers were urged. Resisters were chastised
for wanting to know why the United States was fighting for the
"liberation" of a country that, when free, denied political rights and
decent living conditions to the majority of its population. Predict-
ably, we were labeled "radical" for suggesting that in turn for support the Kuwati government address the subordination of women
and immigrant men. Such concerns were cast aside as politically
irrelevant, militarily extraneous, diplomatically unprecedented, and
culturally insensitive. Even when a war ends, to the extent it does,
the treatment of alternative ideas as dangerous often persists. Even
if they endanger only the excess power of a privileged few, those
few have the status and power to turn democratic challenges into
unpatriotic acts.

Abigail, I should have known when I first read of the American
"revolution" that it must have been an especially difficult time for
women, rather than a time of promise and possibilities. I should
not have been shocked when I read John's reply to your letter, a
reply that ridiculed your priorities from the perspective of a self-
righteous revolutionary who saw some enemies as real and others
as figments of women's no doubt overwrought imaginations. I
wonder about the extent of disappointment—disappointment that
Lucy Stone, in 1855, said is the lot of women.[1] Was the contrast
between decades of freedom for men and women's condition visible to you, even as you devoted much of your life to wife and motherhood? Did you feel more weighted down than usual as events
made clear that this revolution, too, was not for you and your sex
but for the rights of privileged, propertied, educated white men to
run their affairs without having to split the profit with or ask for
permission from England? From "mother" England. Was the rejection of that geographical mother linked to the denial of rights to
real mothers, to women generally? Was England the interfering,
overbearing mother colonists were allowed to despise, a woman
who did not know her place and who must be shown it by the
manly son?

I wonder whether you ever heard of Mary Astell. She wrote some
great works in the seventeenth century, including *Some Reflections
upon Marriage* and *A Serious Proposal to the Ladies*.[2] Over the centu-

ries commentators on Astell have argued that her feminism was limited by her political conservatism, a claim usually based on her failure to take part in the great revolution that was replacing kings with more democratic forms of rule. But I find fascinating Ruth Perry's commentary on such accusations.[3] Perry basically sees that Astell refused to throw her hat in the ring because it was not worth it, as an advocate of women, as what Astell called a lover of her sex. This "revolution" was going to be yet another system of male rule that would come up with yet another justification for women's subordination even while it defended the freedom or participation of more men than had the last one. Astell gives insightful arguments about how aristocracy restrains certain male ambitions. At the very least, Astell makes the point (if we will see it) that the ways in which we have evaluated the worth and consequences of various forms of political rule, political community, and political reform have been incomplete.

Even today, Abigail, it is necessary to make new laws. Or, better, new *codes* of law, as you say. For the problem is not just that law X defines rape too narrowly or that law Y, criminalizing prostitution, needs to be revoked. The problem lies with the code as a whole: its structure, its assumptions, and its effects. Everywhere we see that the "normal" person in law, that around whom laws are built, is a male, as two examples can demonstrate. First, in the 1873 case *Bradwell v. Illinois*,[4] the U.S. Supreme Court upheld an Illinois law denying admission to the state bar—denying women, that is, the right to practice law. In his concurring opinion, Justice Bradley declared that women could not both practice law and embody the "peculiar characteristics, destiny, and mission of woman." "Peculiar" to whom, why, as compared to what, and as determined by whom? If women are "peculiar," is the "norm" of the legal system, the norm determining rights and risks, duties and debts, male? Is the legal system, then, one that cannot, by its structure and nature, serve the interests of women? In the 1961 case *Hoyt v. Florida*,[5] almost a century later, the Supreme Court upheld a Florida law making jury duty mandatory for men and voluntary for women. The concern here was with the compatibility between "the civic duty of jury service . . . [and] her own special responsibilities." As opposed to what other kind of responsibility? The legal system looks at woman as "special," a term whose meanings include "unusual," "peculiar," "different," and "limited." These meanings make clear that, by contrast, the male is the legal norm. It is still necessary for women to make a new Code of Laws. I think you would find some of the work being done today by feminist lawyers and legal theorists (yes, there are many such figures!) pleasing for the ways it challenges fundamental assumptions of our legal system.

I desire you would Remember the Ladies. . . .

Abigail, the part of this exchange of letters that is most cited, in fact the name used to refer to the letter itself, is "Remember the Ladies." Feminists, too, refer to it as such. I always have trouble with the term ladies myself. I cannot strike out from it something inherently unliberating. It calls to me with a list of do's and dont's held up in a shaking fist. In it I see implicit class connotations.

I wonder whether you had any ambivalence about using it. I wonder whether you thought you could get something for yourself by tricking John and others into thinking equality was compatible with women being (traditional) ladies. I wonder, most sadly, whether you meant to exclude from your concern those women who were not ladies, because ladies conveys to me not only rules of conduct meant to undermine women's authority but also hierarchy among women and varieties of forms of women's oppression that also turn women against each other. How far did your concerns extend with regard to class? How much could and would you see, as a female half-member of a new American aristocracy?

The term evokes for me oppressive social structures based on "breeding," "manners," and "nobility." I recall, though, with what grotesque chuckles misogynists of my young adulthood ridiculed "women's libbers" for objecting to the term, as if to do so were to reject civility itself. But true civility does not require women's subordination, and there is nothing "refined" or "delicate" about being dominated. More about power than semantics is involved in the debate.

This call to remember half the population in deliberations on human government assumes it it is possible (probable?) to forget them. Forgotten or never thought of as essential and equal parts of a whole, as individuals with claims sometimes identical to, sometimes at variance with those of others. But not forgotten as if nothing was done that affected them. Women as dependents were part of defining the independent free men.

. . . and be more generous and favourable to them than your ancestors.

Generous??? The treatment of women in the law is the most conditional and unseeing generosity conceivable. *If* you do what we declare is normal, crucial, and desirable for you to do, *then* and only then will we give you what we consider you need, deserve, and desire. If you get married, we will call rape what men other than your husband do when they force you to have sex against your will. But if you are a prostitute, we cannot call whatever happens to you by whomever perpetrates it rape. If you are economically dependent on your husband and he dies, assuming he has been a traditional wage earner, then we will give you social security survivor's benefits so that you can continue to stay home and care for your family. But if you cannot or will not name or find or live with a husband who is the father of your children, do not ask for welfare, for benefits that will enable you to stay home and care for your family.

What men do *for* women is thought of as some gift for which enough appreciation cannot be expressed. What women do *for* men is thought of as women's duty (for which there exists no natural limit). What men do *to* women is thought of as women's fault. What women do *to* men is thought of as unnatural. Published in 1765–1769, Blackstone's *Commentaries on the Laws of England* talked of giving men the right to "chastise" (read: "beat") their wives, to veto any contracts their wives make, to control them, and much more. He repeatedly characterizes such arrangements as "reasonable" and concludes by saying "all of the disabilities she is under are for her benefit, so great a favorite is the female sex of the laws of England." Really, that is just abominable. When male institutions grant women maternity leave, they are heroes. When male institutions grant men leave for prostate surgery, they are doing what they should. Men resent that women get coverage for pregnancy. Women who resent that men get pensions, worker's compensation, company cars, paid vacations, football tickets, lunch write-offs, and secretaries are bitches. What men get they deserve. What women don't get they don't deserve. Male colleagues talking in the hallway about the Monday night football game are building business relationships. Women colleagues talking about Monday night football are unnatural, losing their femininity in the paid labor force just like it was warned would happen. Women colleagues talking about their children are goofing off on company time. Men colleagues talking about their children are both suspect and heroic. Maybe what women need is for men to stop doing us such favors.

Perhaps we really do need no favors at all. "To be favorable" to women is to imperil women, it seems. When an overempowered group favors/supports/helps an underempowered group, they too often do so in unblissful ignorance of the true needs and abilities of the latter, because their position and their interests blind and numb them. When men "favor" women, they too often use their illegitimate power of approval and their ill-gotten means of assisting. Men continue, also, to determine what counts as assistance, what favors women merit or need or desire, and for what purposes. Too, "favor" has elements of indulgence and partiality to it. "Favoring" women reinforces the idea that women, unlike men, need "special" help. But Abigail, perhaps you simply meant that women need men to stop *dis*favoring women, to stop disadvantaging us?

I don't know. Even "generous" originally meant "of noble birth," as if how the "noble" born acted was ample definition of magnanimity. When the haves define unselfishness, that spells trouble for the have-nots. We need men's fairness and men's cooperation, not their so-called gifts and favors.

Do not put such unlimited power into the hands of the Husbands. Remember all Men would be tyrants if they could.

You wrote to Mercy Otis Warren, in explanation of this passage, that "there is a natural propensity in Humane Nature to domination."

Again and again I hear my students hedge, I see them squirm in discomfort, over what to say about men and institutions that have brought harm to women. Abigail, you managed to call them tyrants. You likened their power to that power that is unjust and overbroad. My students want to say that the men misunderstood or did not see or could not help themselves.

I muse a lot about what it is that makes it so difficult to call the power men have tyrannical—typically defined in political science as power that is unchecked, unjustified, not in the interests of those with less power. One factor is reluctance to acknowledge abuse, some desire or need to think that people are basically good at heart. That desire or need certainly is useful for those with more power, for they will be forgiven for their temporary lapses, they will be "understood" rather than confronted, and their acts will often be successfully misrepresented as in the common interest rather than in the interest of a definable part. There seems to be an assumption that acknowledgment of abuse is too . . . too what? Overwhelming? That it is worse, more costly, to acknowledge abuse than to cover it up? This reluctance is even momentarily useful for those with less power, in that it frees them from an obvious obligation to challenge abuse and is one way to see themselves as more than victims.

In fact, you were neither the first nor the last to analyze male-female relationships in terms that were used to analyze political power more generally. Christine de Pizan, Mary Astell, Mary Wollstonecraft, and the authors of the Declaration of Sentiments, among others, all discussed marriage in precisely those terms. It certainly is understandable why women have turned to arguments against tyranny in government, with the hope that anyone who could see the grave defects and dangers of a ruler's power over a citizen would also see the grave injustice and injury of a husband's power over a wife or a child. But somehow it does not always work, maybe even usually it does not. All sorts of attempts are made to show why the analogy doesn't hold, attempts that reveal less about the shortcomings of the analogy than about the interests of those desirous of denying its truths.

I heard you speak from a place that appealed to the common sense. Many days I, too, think the inconsistency of sexism with democratic ideals is so obvious that we need only say it out loud for everything to change. Alas, it is not so.

You tried to make sense for John of the liberation of women by comparing it to the emancipation of a nation, or of "all Nations." You knew that he felt the power of England over the colonies was unjust and tyrannical, and you thought it followed naturally and logically that he would feel the power of men over women was unjust and tyrannical.

Why does that argument so often fail? Why can we not move people committed in one place to ending tyranny and supporting liberty to ally with the women's movement? Is it that they cannot see the similarity? How can it be missed? It seems almost an act of will *not* to see it. But there are a lot of reasons various people have for willing not to see it. Still, some part of it seems to me more than a self-interested act of deception on the part of the hearer, much as I despise John's condescending response to you.

Yesterday I was reading a book to my four- and six-year-old children about manners. Good timing it was, too, for it had been a particularly rough day with them picking on each other. The book opened by talking about how everyone knew there were manners, but some did not know that you should have them at home, too. I looked at Linden, who earlier had pushed Brennin out of his way, and said that what this book is saying is that you know at school that you wouldn't talk to classmates by saying, "Hey, get outta my way!" and shoving them. The same has to be the case at home. Well, that did cause some furrowed brows and pensive stares. The two of them never thought of it that way. Home was somehow different, despite the fact that we explicitly say we treat everyone in all contexts with respect.

John did not see it. Today we would say that "he just doesn't get it." He believed, deeply so, that government was there to protect people's rights and that it was tyrannical for it to usurp those rights. But he was not opposed to tyranny and in support of rights.

He was opposed to some forms of tyranny and in support of certain individuals' possession of certain rights. What a difference. We today have a whole political culture that claims to protect people, but it only protects some, and in some cases. The universality of the language virtually wipes out the very existence of the other forms of oppression, making anyone who speaks out about them seem outrageous, extreme. John yelled with the rest of them, "No taxation without representation!" But he denied the connection between that and women's cry: "No obedience to laws in which we have no voice."

If perticuliar care and attention is not paid to the Laidies we are ◦ *determined to foment a Rebelion, and will not hold ourselves bound by any Laws in which we have no voice, or Representation.*

Some have called this threat to foment a rebellion "half-jesting."[6] I hope it was not. It is one of my favorite parts.

Abigail, you had restraint in your words even at times when I could feel the intensity of your anger. You asked men to "Remember the Ladies" and to be more "generous and favourable." But the rage, the righteous rage, you did let out at times, and for that I am grateful. I especially liked that you threatened men with rebellion and credited yourself and other women with the power to free yourselves. Two hundred twenty years after you wrote, the words of yours that are most remembered are not those threatening to overthrow male tyrants but those that sound almost polite and definitely proper: your plea to "Remember the Ladies." You might find it unsurprising that two hundred twenty years after you wrote, those of us who labor for women's equality are still called to task for the tone of our words. "Don't be so demanding," we are told. "Stop bashing men," we are urged. Such obnoxious demands I know are an attempt to divert the debate about women's oppression into one over manners. Further, what we are chided for is being unladylike, when precisely what we are challenging is women's restriction in work, recreation, language, and family to what men deem ladylike! Men know the power of powerful words—as you so clearly saw, the language of struggle, despotism, and inde-

pendence the colonies used helped their cause, and men objecting
to women's language of independence against unjust authority is
an attempt to undermine women's cause.

Let me tell you something that would make you proud. You lived
on after your death in ways that would please you. On July 4, 1876,
the United States was celebrating its centennial. Some women,
however, declined simply to go along with a celebration of freedom, given that they still had fewer rights than male citizens. (This
was, by the way, neither the first nor the last time we would find
eras, anniversaries, etc., marked according to what they meant for
men. So-called ages of enlightenment, for example, have been dark
ages for women, just as national liberations have often come at the
cost of women's freedom. The things are not only misnamed. They
are ways of wiping out women's experiences and tactics for denying the connection between the liberation of some and the failing
conditions of others.) Five women, headed by Susan B. Anthony,
interrupted the official celebration in Philadelphia and read the
Declaration of Rights for Women by the National Woman Suffrage
Association. Toward the end the document said, "From the beginning of the century, when Abigail Adams, the wife of one president
and mother of another, said, 'We will not hold ourselves bound to
obey laws in which we have no voice or representation,' until now,
woman's discontent has been steadily increasing, culminating
nearly thirty years ago in a simultaneous movement among the
women of the nation, demanding the right of suffrage."[7]

*That your Sex are Naturally Tyrannical is a Truth so thoroughly
established as to admit of no dispute . . .*

This is odd language to a reader in the last years of the twentieth
century. Today we almost scrupulously avoid speaking of the "nature" of any group, with the understanding that to do so is to remove the element of agency and responsibility, deny the possibility
of change, and ignore a group's internal diversity. In fact, my students define as male bashing comments such as yours, precisely
because it lumps all men together and in a negative way. But I take

it that you were using natural in a common eighteenth-century sense of the term.

Natural tyranny referred to the untamed, unrestrained, unguided appetites of asocial or antisocial individuals living outside a political community. The many aspects of political life—such as laws, customs, and education—were expected to "humanize" the "beast." Add to this understanding of nature the knowledge of the tyrannical acts of (privileged) men against many "other" groups, and the "indisputability" of your statement becomes clearer.

Have we lost anything by moving away from such political thinking and language? What we need, I think, is an understanding of how every political context shapes and socializes in some way, including a "state of nature." Whatever appetites, hormones, or character individuals begin with, those are given meaning and are either rewarded or discouraged, as a (dominant) political culture determines is appropriate. Today antifeminists are most confident referring to arguments about men's "natural" hormonal aggression that rightly results, for example, in men holding leadership positions in business and politics. Your point could be used, as can others, to argue that only a particular society can determine the acceptable range for and responses to men's (supposed) hormonal aggression. Just as near-sighted people who can afford to generally wear glasses to "correct" their vision, so a community could decide that hormonal levels in men, if proven to contribute to male domination of women, should be "corrected" for the common good.

. . . but such of you as wish to be happy willingly give up the harsh title of Master for the more tender and endearing one of Friend.

The 1632 document *The Lawes Resolutions of Women's Rights* describes a husband as a woman's "superior; her companion, her master," as if a master could unproblematically also be a friend.[8] (Though it is true that Aristotle, too, spoke of a form of friendship between unequals, including friendship between "any sort of ruler towards the one he rules," he at least considered such to be inferior to friendship between peers.[9]) I now know it to be a long-standing argument of women that a man should be not the lord of his wife but the two should be each other's companions. It is a claim made by Astell, Wollstonecraft, and Mill, to name just a few.

It is odd enough that women should be trained to gear all their hopes and dreams toward the time they marry. It is romanticized and enforced, with the romanticization often conveniently covering the enforcement. But the peculiarity is not only that all women should have this single and singular fate, a fate that is a relationship rather than a fulfillment of individualized ambitions, but that the relationship toward which all women aim demands their subservience. We work so that we may be ruled. We make ourselves pleasing so that we may be ignored and ridiculed and abused. Astonishing, really.

My students often resist the idea that a husband could or would really be a master over his wife. Though most of them hope some day to be lawyers, they resort here to arguing that law is irrelevant, without influence over "private" lives. They manage to envision someone without property rights, without the right to vote, without occupational freedom, without equal educational opportunities, in general with inferior civil rights and second-class citizenship, as nonetheless the equal of her husband, who not only might have all the rights and opportunities explicitly denied her but might also have power over her granted by law (control of her property, the right to abuse her physically).

It seems to be so important for them to assert that nothing truly awful, fundamentally unequal, occurred or occurs between the sexes that even a familiar belief in something like the connection between the right to vote and equality becomes debatable. They insist that men could be both master and friend, that the structure of a relationship is unconnected to its content, that women were not and are not disempowered in ways that affect their daily lives. When these young people encounter other realities, they run from political to individual explanations ("I didn't . . ."; "She could have . . ."), protecting not themselves, not women in general, but the status quo. Sometimes I feel infuriated by this cycle; sometimes listening breaks my heart.

Why then, not put it out of the power of the vicious and the Lawless to use us with cruelty and indignity with impunity.

Here is one of those places where it becomes painfully obvious that the government was not established to protect women against the ills most likely to befall them. Your question is so simple. It takes as fact that many women are treated cruelly by their husbands, that such treatment is an affront to women's human dignity, and that presently men suffer no consequences for their cruel behavior. It wonders why fundamental law cannot punish men for such behavior. Such a question really is in line with much of the thinking of your time on government, at least from some perspectives. Liberal theory rebutted the need and justice of certain forms of governmental power. It created a story that said that people without the common authority of a government were not safe or happy but that all the government they needed could be had by a representative government that was checked by the people and that checked itself by dividing into mutually suspicious branches. It had to be checked to make sure that its task of creating the conditions in which people may lead free and independent lives was accomplished and that it didn't try to do more than that. So here you come, Abigail, and you ask the obvious question. Paraphrasing, I believe you say, "Women's freedom is undermined by the abuse of power that men may exert over them in marriage. Since you declare that government is supposed to create conditions for people to be free, so it follows that government should do what is appropriate to stop men's abusive treatment of women." But it turns out that that was not what was bargained for. What men ended up justifying was government regulation in the public sphere. They were adamant that government power should stop at the border of the private. And so for men it became essential that freedom meant no government intrusion into the home. And for women no government intrusion into the home meant that there would be no assistance in stopping domestic violence, wife battering. The very ideology that might have been of use to women, that you knew could be of use to women, ended up being used to justify government turning its back on women.

Sometimes, as I made clear earlier, I read your words as reflecting and contributing to class bias. But here I think in fact you present a challenge to classism. For you now use terms such as vicious and cruel as linked not with class or birth but with behavior. You revealed that men of all classes could be vicious.

What counts as cruel? Compare your statement with an 1875 law case *In re Goodell.* Judge Ryan upheld the practice of banning women from admission to the bar of Wisconsin largely on the basis of their domestic obligations. He spoke thus to women without such obligations: "The *cruel* chances of life sometimes baffle both sexes, and may leave women free from the peculiar duties of their sex." His words to such cruelly treated women? "These may need employment," but they will not find it in the practice of law, since such employment is "derogatory to their sex and its proprieties, [and] inconsistent with the good order of society."[10]

Men of Sense in all Ages abhor those customs which treat us only as the vassals of your Sex.

You make an interesting reference here to men who abhor women's subordination. Strategically, it made sense for you to tell the all-male governers (including your husband) that if they stood for (some) rights for women they would not be the first, that they had male predecessors. Although "firsts" are sometimes applauded, they are more often mistrusted, for they exist as fearsome challengers to "tradition," to "the way we have always done things." We want to fight for independence in this revolution, but again the note of wariness emerges.

Erasing the history, the tradition, of women's resistance to male domination has some obvious ties to the maintenance of patriarchy. Erasing the history, the tradition, of male resistance, has perhaps less obvious consequences.

The first day of class in recent semesters I put a series of quotes on an overhead that discuss the history of legal discrimination, the role law has played in perpetuating (rather than eliminating) inequality. After going over the content, I ask my students which quotes they think are from women, which from men, and why. In general they tend to assume that any assertion of women's subordination comes from a woman. The exception tends to be that quotes discussing sexism's negative impact on men are sometimes thought to be by men. Just to make a point, all the quotes I use are from men. And more than a few eyebrows are raised and furrowed when I tell them so. Think of what their expectations reveal!

Regard us then as Beings placed by providence under your protection and in immitation of the Supreem Being make use of that power only for our happiness.

Abigail, why did you talk of women being under men's protection? "Under" someone's protection is still "under" them. The arrangement marks the "protected" as incapable of self-protection, which then gets turned into evidence of all sorts of other incapabilities. Similarly, it marks men as capable not only of taking care of themselves but as being the caretakers of others.

In the debate over protective legislation in the early twentieth century, Crystal Eastman wrote:

> To blot out of every law book in the land, to sweep out of every dusty court-room, to erase from every judge's mind that centuries-old precedent as to woman's inferiority and dependence and need for protection, to substitute for it at one blow the simple new precedent of equality, that is a fight worth making if it takes ten years.[11]

Ten years?! Eastman, reporting on the action of the Women's Freedom League, wrote that the organization's position was that "any special protective restrictions can only undermine women's chance for equality." She summarized their view thus: "all restrictive legislation in regard to women's work is engineered by men who do not wish to have women's full competition in their particular trades, and in the interests of women should be uncompromisingly opposed."[12] In the language of the late twentieth century, Zillah Eisenstein wrote thus of protection: "Protection involves relations of power and assumes that those who need protection have less power or are unequal to another's power."[13]

Perhaps what you meant to do was to create room for a notion, and a practice, of benevolent and caring protection? It is so clear that you knew how men had misused the illegitimate power they held over women, your comment is neither naive nor based on a refusal to see. I think it makes sense to read your words as contesting what protection actually means. For you are contrasting then current practices with true protection of women's rights, not protection of individual women by individual men but legal protection of the rights of all women and men. Perhaps today the idea of protection has a history it did not have in 1776, Abigail. If so, that history, I believe, tells us to find other practices and other language.

The language of protection has been used to make laws that discriminate against women appear palatable, justifiable, even necessary. But such laws have "protected" women out of jobs. Protective legislation becomes a code of conduct that dictates what women should be doing, when, and where. These rules are then used *against* women who fail to conform. So what really gets protected is not women but those gendered codes of conduct that reinforce women's inequality. The language of protection has lulled our critical faculties to sleep.

Truly, though, none of us survive unprotected, in isolation. Male infants left untended die as surely as do female infants. Studies today show married men to be happier and healthier than single men, though that does not hold for women. Men have in fact been protected by women. If that sounds strange to the ear, perhaps it shows how gendered the very idea of protection is, and thus how important it is to leave such concepts and words behind.

As to your extraordinary Code of Laws, I cannot but laugh.

I cringe when I read this, every time. The utter arrogance, the disrespect, the haughty tone of the smug superior. A demand for women's inclusion is extraordinary, meaning that women's exclusion is ordinary, normal. Taking women into account in forming a government is so ridiculous that it is humorous. Women's rights are laughable; women are laughable. Men are serious and to be taken seriously. And women are supposed to be entertaining, so it is almost fitting to be entertained by whatever it is they say. Nothing women say will be beyond laughter. Nothing. I feel that in the pit of my stomach. It is watching men react to me as if I wasn't there, or wasn't there as a full human being, or was there only as it suited them. It is, I think, one of those moments when it is possible to see easily and clearly what male dominance really amounts to.

We have been told that our Struggle has loosened the bands of Government every where. That Children and Apprentices were disobedient—that schools and Colledges were grown turbulent—that Indians slighted their Guardians and Negroes grew insolent to their Masters. But your Letter was the first Intimation that another Tribe more numerous and powerfull than all the rest were grown discontented.

I was taught from the time I was a child through my graduate school education that the American revolution was about freedom and equality. And yet John makes so clear in his response to you that the revolution was a partial one. The work he and his friends are engaged in is a "Struggle" that is meant to "[loosen] the bands of Government [not] every where" but only some where. There are still to be governers and governed. For the governed who are not colonists resisting rulers who are not England, take note: disobedience can be punished; turbulence must be controlled; insolence is an affront that cannot be tolerated; to slight those who do not deserve to be slighted is an injustice. Such actions are not justified, John says, are not like his.

This is rather too coarse a Compliment but you are so saucy, I wont blot it out.

In a letter to Mercy Otis Warren, April 27, 1776, you wrote, "He is very sausy to me in return for a List of Female Grievances which I transmitted to him." You use the same term *saucy* to describe his response that he used to describe your appeal. And yet it is a sexist term—did you know that, and were you using it to make your point?

Depend upon it, We know better than to repeal our Masculine systems.

I often tell my students that the claim that there is such a a thing as a patriarchy is not so new (they think such analysis was born in the 1960s, in women's studies departments of universities). Not only have feminists been speaking of it for centuries, but even defenders of the status quo have been willing sometimes to call it what it is. John saw something he could name a "Masculine system." The "our" before it is noteworthy. Did he mean to make it yours too? Did he mean that men understood it in some common way? My students bristle at the idea that male domination is some sort of conspiracy. When they think of a conspiracy, they think of a small group sitting around together plotting how to gain something for themselves at the expense of others. I always tell them (only half in jest, to make a point, of course) that I am a fan of conspiracy theories. I do not usually think of men sitting around trying to figure out how to put the screws to women—though in fact I think that happens every day. I think of the fact that men support each other in upholding a coordinated system that benefits them and hurts others.

Altho they are in full Force, you know they are little more than Theory. We dare not exert our Power in its full Latitute.

In other words, you have no valid complaint, Abigail. You are complaining about something that does not exist in practice, in fact, but in theory only. Another dismissal.

John says here that men do not exert their power in its full latitude. What does it mean for them to exert their superior power at all, even to less than the maximum possible? Does this mean that things could be worse, so women should be thankful? Does possession of the capacity for full exertion mean nothing? And is it never taken advantage of by any? It seems clear to me, Abigail, that whom John is worried about and whom he is leaving out differ dramatically from the objects of your concern.

We are obliged to go fair, and softly, and in Practice you know We are the subjects. We have only the Name of Masters, and rather than give up this, which would compleatly subject Us to the Despotism of the Peticoat . . .

Not only is male power only a reality in theory, in law, now John goes further: despite legal superiority, men are really the subjects of women, who are fearful or fickle sovereigns against whom men would not "dare" to exert their own power.

This is a fantastic line of argument, as long as we understand the root of *fantastic* to be "based in fantasy." John is saying that male superiority in legal codes does not mean inequality for women. But gender equality in legal codes would mean the subordination of men.

The best sense I can make of John's claim is this: Women have power over men in some (unspecified) places or via some (unspecified) means. So men would be subjected to women were men to give up their power in other places. Generally such arguments are based on an appeal to women's sexuality, through which they can supposedly control men.

Although women's use of their sexuality as a weapon against men may look like female power to men, it often looks like alienation from one's sexuality to women, and limitation of it for survival, to have some voice against men. To me this does not look like a case for equal but different forms of power for the two sexes. It looks like an indictment of patriarchy, which is revealed as filled with desperation, alienation, and power plays. Perhaps Mary Astell has the best response to John's position:

> She must be a Fool with a witness, who can believe a Man, Proud and Vain as he is, will lay his boasted Authority, the Dignity and Prerogative of his Sex, one Moment at her Feet, but in prospect of taking it up again to more advantage; he may call himself her Slave a few days, but it is only in order to make her his all the rest of his Life.[14]

Although John has just admitted at least that male dominance exists in law, he does not then say we should repeal it, though he does imply that such a change is possible. On the contrary. Just because male supremacy is (supposedly) in theory only, do not conclude that we will alter it at that level.

What an image: "the Despotism of the Peticoat." Do you know that Wollstonecraft was called a "hyena in petticoats"? Do you know that men who "pursue" women are called "skirt-chasers"? A student of mine had a great response when she read this part of John's letter. "Here Abigail is talking about laws, power, and politics," she said, "and John starts talking about her underwear!" I actually hadn't thought of it in those terms, but my student's comment reveals from another angle how John is ignoring the substance of your letter and how he is defining women in terms having nothing to do with citizenship or humanity.

I hope General Washington, and all our brave Heroes would fight. I am sure every good Politician would plot, as long as he would against Despotism, Empire, Monarchy, Aristocracy, Oligarchy, or Ochlocracy.

Again we see more of John's ridicule. The idea of Washington fending off women in petticoats! Nonetheless, John was making clear the still popular idea that there is something unpatriotic about women making demands of their government and something unjust about any power women make claim to. Women with power are (m)aligned with every form of government except that which at the time of his letter was most legitimate: democracy.

P.S. I hope it pleases you to know that many today read your words, take them seriously, and wrestle over how various passages should be understood. I am one of those readers. I have learned from you and with you. I will always reread you with an image of you in my mind as someone with strength and sense struggling, at times uneasily, on a battlefield not of her own making.

Notes

1. In her remarks to the 1855 National Woman's Rights Convention in Cincinnati, Ohio, Stone said, "In education, in marriage, in religion, in everything, disappointment is the lot of woman. It shall be the business of

my life to deepen this disappointment in every woman's heart until she bows down to it no longer." *Feminism: The Essential Historical Writings*, ed. Miriam Schneir (New York: Vintage, 1972), 106.

2. Astell also wrote *Letters Concerning the Love of God* (1695), *Moderation Truly Stated* (1704), *A Fair Way with the Dissenters and Their Patrons* (1704), *An Impartial Enquiry into the Causes of Rebellion and Civil War in this Kingdom* (1704), *The Christian Religion as Profess'd by a Daughter of the Church of England* (1705), and *Bartlemy Fair* (1709).

3. Ruth Perry, *Mary Astell: An Early English Feminist* (Chicago: University of Chicago Press, 1986).

4. 83 U.S. 130, 21 L.Ed. 442.

5. 368 U.S. 57, 82 S.Ct. 159, 7 L.Ed.2d 118.

6. Alice Rossi, *The Feminist Papers*, 7.

7. See "Declaration of Rights for Women," in *We, the Other People*, ed. Philip Foner (Urbana: University of Illinois Press, 1976), esp. 111–12. Also see Frederick Douglass' 1852 "What to the Slave is the Fourth of July?"

8. *Women in American Law*, vol. 1, ed. Marlene Stein Wortman (New York: Holmes & Meier, 1985), 27.

9. Aristotle, *Nichomachean Ethics*, Book VIII.

10. *In re Goodell*, emphasis added, *Women in American Law*, vol. 1, 248–51, esp. 250.

11. Crystal Eastman, "Feminists Must Fight," in *On Women & Revolution*, ed. Blanche Wiesen Cook (Oxford: Oxford University Press, 1978), 161.

12. Crystal Eastman, "English Feminists and Special Labor Laws for Women," in *On Women & Revolution*, 163, 164.

13. Zillah Eisenstein, *Feminism and Sexual Equality: Crisis in Liberal America* (New York: Monthly Review Press, 1984), 176.

14. Mary Astell, "Reflections upon Marriage," in Perry, *Mary Astell*, 100.

Thomas versus Hill

Here again you will read multiple conversations. The first is one I set up between different sets of reactions to the Thomas–Hill hearings. The second is between my own choices of what to focus on in talking about the hearings, and the sometimes different responses of women of color.

A friend who long ago read some of my work on Rousseau said she was struck by how ahistorical it was, how someone could read it and not know, for example, who the king of France was. I realized in rereading my comments on the Thomas-Hill hearings that someone could read them and not know the race of either party. In both cases what got left out takes away from what got included.

And where the words of women are crying to be heard, we must each of us recognize our responsibility to seek those words out, to read them and share them and examine them in their pertinence to our lives. That we not hide behind the mockeries of separations that have been imposed upon us and which so often we accept as our own. For instance, "I can't possibly teach Black women's writing—their experience is so different from mine." Yet how many years have you spent teaching Plato and Shakespeare and Proust?

Audre Lorde, "The Transformation of Silence into Language and Action"

10

❦ ❦ ❦

Thomas versus Hill: Rethinking My Commentary in Light of Writings by African American Feminists

As a teacher of law-related courses, I usually pay attention to Supreme Court nominations, of which there have been several in recent years. As a feminist I have paid increased attention lately, knowing that though laws neither make nor break a revolution, several currently contested laws have dramatic effects on women's daily lives; aspects of laws regulating abortion, family leave, AFDC eligibility, sexual harassment, comparable worth, and discrimination based on pregnancy are among those that continue to be negotiated and renegotiated.

During that part of the Clarence Thomas nomination process to the Supreme Court that revolved around the charge that he had sexually harassed female coworkers, I was incredibly tense. Some of that was no doubt the result of a nontelevision watcher being glued for endless hours to the screen. Some of it was concern about the final outcome. Some of it was the incessant questioning I got about my views on the particular incident involving Anita Hill and on the general phenomenon of harassment. But I think that most of the tension was the result of a feeling that the hearings, the reactions they generated, and the coverage they received not only put

Hill on trial, or, less, Thomas, but feminist political analysis. This very public prime-time trial would end in some sort of verdict about feminism, a verdict that would impact feminist politics for at least the near future. I found myself tracking what the process revealed about the current status of the women's movement and what it would itself contribute to that movement.

As the hearings appeared to be nearing their end and the Senate vote got closer, a group of faculty and staff quickly put together a public panel discussion on various aspects of sexual harassment and the hearings. Seeming to confirm my sense of things, this informal, in-house panel drew the largest audience of university and community people that I have seen at any similar event at Purdue. For my part, I lined up various aspects of the then still ongoing "incident" as either a "positive" or "negative" comment on or contribution to the women's movement. Most of that 1991 presentation is in section I here, with some changes in order and organization of ideas. My remarks constituted a conversation between different elements of or perspectives on the events and between the hearings and feminist politics.

Now years later, I have constructed another conversation, this time between my own past remarks about Thomas–Hill and the clearly more race-conscious responses to it as represented in two rich anthologies: *Race-ing Justice, En-gendering Power: Essays on Anita Hill, Clarence Thomas, and the Construction of Social Reality*, and *Court of Appeal: The Black Community Speaks Out on the Racial and Sexual Politics of Clarence Thomas vs. Anita Hill.*[1] I wanted to do this work as a way to introduce more voices into my analysis, to allow that introduction to involve confrontations with my own silencing of issues at the intersection of race and gender politics, and to explore and appreciate how ideas and practices change when one moves among or between racial standpoints. This second dialogue constitutes section II.

As Toni Morrison portrays it, the hearings generated diverse and almost endless conversations, and those I try to capture are neither exhaustive nor even necessarily representative.

> But most of all, people talked to one another. There are passionate, sometimes acrimonious discussions between mothers and daughters,

fathers and sons, husbands and wives, siblings, friends, acquaintances, colleagues with whom, now, there is reason to embrace or to expel from their close circle. Sophisticated legal debates merge with locker-room guffaws; poised exchanges about the ethics and moral responsibilities of governance are debased by cold indifference to individual claims and private vulnerabilities. Organizations and individuals call senators and urge friends to do the same—providing opinions and information, threatening, cajoling, explaining positions, or simply saying, "Confirm! Reject! Vote yes. Vote no."[2]

Section I

1. On the negative

The panicky reaction of some people to Hill's accusations has been "No man is safe!" Somehow focus turned to potentially endangered males rather than real injured women.

On the positive

Journalist Bob Maynard noted that men with serious career ambitions would have to think differently about how they address women. Expressions of male vulnerability of this sort—the sort that actually challenge men rather than women to change—is *not* usual. Even when men think or know their conduct is questionable or wrong, they can generally be secure that few question it or question it effectively. This feeling of vulnerability leading to amended practices is potentially quite constructive.

2. On the negative

Antifeminists conjured up one of their favorite and most reliable images—the lying, vindictive woman. One of the reasons, that is, that "no man is safe" is that any woman can and will just make up allegations like Hill's. Unfortunately, the image of the untrustworthy, dishonest, vicious woman was more familiar to many than were alternative readings of the situation.

On the positive

On the positive, years of scholarship and activism show that this is what has been said about virtually every crime in which men are usually the perpetrators and women are usually the victims. It has been said about stranger rape, date rape, marital rape, incest, and spouse abuse, for example. The assumption is that women habitually lie and somehow gain by such lying. But we know—we *know*—the truth is that when women make such accusations the women themselves end up on trial. And women know that. That is why it is estimated that for crimes in which women are usually the victims, 90 percent of women do not report them. Feminists can now insist that we focus on what we can do to make the workplace and the home and the police station and the courtroom safer for that 90 percent, instead of paying disproportionate attention to false reports, which, at worst, do not exceed the number of false reports for other crimes.

3. On the negative side

Some people characterized behavior such as that described by Hill as "a matter of interpretation" and sexual harassment complaints as insoluble "he said, she said" problems, as if those aren't the kinds of problems judges and juries face and resolve everyday in every area of the law.

Many men have responded to the hearings by saying not only that *anyone* can be accused of illegal behavior but that *anything* can be construed as sexual harassment. They are saying that they are not sure what they can and cannot do anymore, that they are confused, even anxious. Most troubling, this response denies that there is a distinct practice called sexual harassment, since anything can be and supposedly will be called sexual harassment. Thus, sexual harassment is not even a real, distinctive problem.

But on the other hand

More women are comfortable letting men wrestle with this, rather than exempting them or trying to solve it for them. There is no way to get men to change their behavior that does not entail self-reflection and reconsideration of one's attitudes and acts. The very fact of confusion shows how privileged some men have been—how utterly unaccountable they have been to women, how little they have thought about the way they treat women. Women's training in accommodation is self-defeating; women asking and demanding of men that they rethink their own behavior truly is significant progress.

4. On the negative

Another reaction to Hill's accusations has been "What is she making such a big deal about? So what if he did say those things? Men say things like that all the time. If women want to be in the workplace, they should get used to it."

On the positive

For those who need it, there is an acknowledgment in this reaction that, as feminists have argued, sexism is pervasive. Men say things like that "all the time." And women are expected to tolerate it, all the time. Too, the workplace is revealed as built by and for men, with women marked as unwelcome, intrusive and unreasonably demanding. For to whom is sexual harassment "no big deal"?

But now women are coming forward to talk about the extent and costs both of being harassed and of trying to tolerate it, costs that range from stress-related ailments and low self-esteem to lost promotions, lost jobs, humiliation, and violation. And better still, women are being heard to say we cannot and will not play by the old unwritten sexist rules of the workplace. The sexualization and objectification of women can have no place in the new rules—again, it is the workplace, and not just women, being required to change. Perhaps some space was even created for male dissention from previously approved male harassing behavior.

5. On the negative side

Questioning the hearing themselves, people said they didn't think Thomas's private behavior was rightly a matter of concern in determining his fitness for public office.

But on the positive side

A New York Times/CBS poll on October 11, 1991 showed that two-thirds of those surveyed said if it were to be shown that Thomas did harass Hill, they thought that sufficient to disqualify him. And that's progress. Because one of the difficult things about sexism is that whatever happens to women because they're women, like rape and harassment, it's said women ask for it and even enjoy it. With such a defense, rape and harassment aren't problems.

Many of us know, and the law now reflects, that sexual harassment is a form of sex discrimination. It is a question not of the perpetrator's personal predilections but of equal opportunity, a political issue.[3]

We also know enough not to let the mantle of privacy be used as a way to avoid accountability for abuse and unfairness. In the case of Thomas and Hill, we see that a manifestation of women's subordination—sexualization in the paid labor force—is actually considered a problem for her and something to hold against him. The harasser is not just a good old boy having a little fun without hurting anyone. That's progress, because before we can eliminate women's oppression, we first have to convince people it's a problem.

6. On the negative side

Senator Joseph Biden, chair of the Senate Judiciary Committee, did not fully discuss the harassment charges with all the panel members once he knew of them, and the partly informed committee never questioned Thomas about them. Of those members of the Judiciary Committee that did see the complaint by Hill, not one deemed it serious enough to deserve thorough investigation before voting on Thomas's confirmation. Many weren't sure an allegation of harassment merited postponing the original October 8 vote, a delay that would allow (some) investigation of the charges. And many in the Senate seemed more concerned, more outraged, over news leaks, "political ploys," and broken rules than with harassment.

But, on the positive side

As a result of these and similar acts, it actually became a legitimate part of the conversation to ask whether an all-male, all-white Judiciary Committee and a 98 percent male Senate might have a certain bias. Senator Paul Simon admitted "a lack of sensitivity toward women's concerns" in such a body. Talk about the reality and power of the old boy network made more sense to more people.

7. On the positive side

During this process we got to see where women's presence at varied levels in diverse institutions does make a difference. We saw the potential power of the gender-based anger of women journalists who, for example, questioned Senator Pete DeConcini about why he seemed automatically to believe Thomas and to disbelieve Hill. We saw those reporters give the most extensive treatment of sexual harassment ever to hit the major papers. We heard of a letter sent to the Senate leadership signed by seventy women law professors asking for a delay in the vote on Thomas. We heard of black women law professors and lobbyists meeting with Senate majority leader George Mitchell. Senator Biden consulted with women's groups on the issue of harassment. The senators had to cope with an activism they could not ignore. They learned about women's political power, their anger, and perhaps even the cause of the anger, as a *New York Times* editorial put it.[4]

And yet, on the negative side

People thought they were defending Hill when they said, as a colleague of hers at Oklahoma said, "It is not fair to say she is an activist in the national, ideological community,"[5] as if activism was inherently suspect. Similarly, the *New York Times* praised her thus: "She was an activist without rancor, refusing to point fingers or lay blame." As if it would be inherently suspect to blame someone for violating the law and a person's integrity.

8. On the negative side

Oh so many people said they couldn't understand why Hill kept her job after she was harassed or why she didn't report the harassment. They couldn't believe anyone could say the things Thomas allegedly said and, best of all, coming from Senator Alan Simpson, could not accept that the judicial system might not have worked well for a victim of harassment ten years ago or today if she did report it.

On the positive side

It became an accepted part of the discussion to argue that, because of sexism, men and women are trained differently and frequently see things differently. "They just don't get it" emerged as a common and telling refrain about men. But best of all, *getting* women's viewpoints mattered. People were interested in how women understand and experience harassment and in what men or the popular perception of harassment might be missing. The ancient legal standard of the "reasonable man" is being pushed aside to make room for the reasonable woman.[6]

9. On the negative side

What finally motivated the senators to reconsider the charges against Thomas was concern over reelection and over the reputation of the Senate and the Supreme Court, not some deep and long-standing commitment to sexual equality.

But on the positive side

A "woman's issue" had the ability to bring the institutions of the Senate and the Supreme Court into question.

10. Finally, on the negative side

An official said the administration's plan was "to prevent this from turning into a referendum on 2000 years of male dominance and sexual harassment."[7]

On the positive side

In that statement we actually have administration officials admitting to millennia of male dominance and sexual harassment!

Section II

> For any kind of lasting illumination the focus must be on the history routinely ignored or played down or unknown.
> Toni Morrison, *Race-ing Justice*

What I present now are insights I have gained from reading commentary by African Americans on the Hill-Thomas hearings that I would incorporate into my presentation if I were giving it today. I learned three main things in my readings: first, none of the insights was beyond me. That is, had I worked harder, or thought more inclusively, or talked to a wider range of people, I could have come up with at least many of these points. Whites like myself, supposedly committed to racial equality and inclusion, cannot sit passively and wait for people of color to enlighten us. Men can see sexism. Whites can see and name race-specific aspects of an event. That does not mean we know as much, or as deeply, or that we can know it in isolation—without listening and acting. It does mean that we cannot play stupid and cannot absolve ourselves from responsibility. Second, in my readings I came across many many writers who made some of the same points I did. There is not necessary antagonism between those working for sexual equality and those working for racial equality, as the daily lives of women of color alone should tell. But third, those points that I did not make that I grasped better through my reading of African Americans truly did make fuller sense of the hearings. We need very much to learn from one another, to engage in conversation.

Thus, I would now add at least the following:

11. On one hand

In telling his life story and in responding to Hill's charges, Thomas made references to an all-too-real history of racial victimization in the United States, and rightly noted destructive myths about black men that still thrive, especially myths about their supposedly aggressive, rapacious sexuality.

But on the other hand,

As Homi Bhabha explains, when Thomas brought up "the figure of the lynched black man," he was, with much success, "divert[ing] attention from the content or substance of Anita Hill's sexual-harassment charges." Here "the vivid imagery of an antiracist language [was used] to silence the feminist discourse on sexual harassment."[8] His victimization rather than hers became the subject.

Thomas also ignored that black men were not hung for the rape (no less the sexual harassment) of black women but of white women. He ignored that there were myths about the hypersexuality of black women that undermined Hill's credibility as much as myths about the sexuality of black men undermined his.

12. On the one hand

Every stereotype of "woman" and of "black woman" was used against Hill.

Before the eyes of a nation, a tenured law professor beloved by her students was transformed into an evil, opportunistic harpy; a deeply religious Baptist was turned into a sick and delusional woman possessed by Satan and in need of exorcism; this youngest of thirteen children from a loving family became a frustrated spinster longing for the attentions of her fast-track superior, bent on exacting a cruel revenge for his rejection.[9]

And it was possible for this to happen because of how securely sexist and racist stereotypes remain in place, and how recent the conversations that challenge them really are.

But on the other hand

Hill's approach, in fact her very existence, also challenged numerous stereotypes of black women. An ambitious, successful, professional, Republican black woman presented her case with obvious integrity. She was not silenced and she did not blame herself, nor was she "[t]he surly black wife with a frying pan in her hand."[10] Throughout the coverage of the hearings and the commentaries that followed them, Hill was described as "intelligent," "impressively self-possessed," and "courageous." Her challenge of Thomas's behavior also reminded those who needed reminding that contrary to the stereotype, blacks, like members of all groups, differ from one another in their values, ideas, personal histories, and political priorities.

13. On one hand

A black woman challenged a black man before a room of white men with the power to affect his fate. This intraracial episode amounted, for some, to washing dirty linen in public, even to Hill being a traitor to her race.

But on the other hand

Perhaps here a black woman respectfully and successfully challenged that aspect of their partnership with black men that demands the silencing of black women for the supposed sake of their race. Any group that silences some of its members and claims to do so in the interest of all is excluding those silenced members from the "all." As Nellie McKay explains it:

[P]erhaps the greatest beneficiaries . . . of Anita Hill's publicly uttering her allegations . . . are millions of black women for whom her
action represented a further breaking of the bonds of generations of
black women's silence on and denial of their differences with black
men, because of gender issues, and their right to be full human beings
despite the conflicts of race and sex.[11]

Morrison adds, "the time for undiscriminating racial unity has
passed. A conversation, a serious exchange between black men and
women, has begun in a new arena, and the contestants defy the
mold."[12]

14. Finally, on the negative

The hearings and the uproar they generated revealed America's
continuing difficulty with "thinking about gender and race simultaneously," as Nell Painter puts it.[13] Many wanted to force Hill to
choose between a feminist loyalty to white women and a racial loyalty to black men. As Christine Stansell says, "for historians the
Thomas–Hill hearings echoed an old, sad story . . . [of t]he painful
division between antiracism and feminism."[14]

On the positive

An examination of racism in the women's movement, while neither unhalting nor finished, many years ago moved "from margin
to center"[15] in feminist scholarship and activism. This work enables
someone like "Crenshaw, resounding in her absolute opposition to
the nomination, [to emphasize] the racism and misogyny that lay
intertwined at its very heart."[16]

My final assessment of what the hearings had to say about feminism matches Stansell's:

The fact that Anita Hill testified at all, and that her accusations had
such a stunning impact on national politics, testifies to the continuing
power of the American women's movement, however diffused it may
be.[17]

Notes

1. *Race-ing Justice, En-gendering Power*, ed. Toni Morrison (New York: Pantheon, 1992); *Court of Appeal*, ed. Robert Chrisman and Robert Allen (New York: Ballantine, 1992).

2. Morrison, *Race-ing Justice*, viii-ix.

3. The U.S. Supreme Court first declared sexual harassment to be a violation of Title VII of the 1964 Civil Rights Act in the 1986 case *Meritor v. Vinson*. Citing a lower court decision in *Henson v. Dundee*, the Court said, "Sexual harassment which creates a hostile or offensive environment for members of one sex is every bit the arbitrary barrier to sexual equality at the workplace that racial harassment is to racial equality. Surely, a requirement that a man or woman run a gauntlet of sexual abuse in return for the privilege of being allowed to work and make a living can be as demeaning and disconcerting as the harshest of racial epithets."

4. "Finally, a Proper Hearing," *New York Times*, October 10, 1991, A16.

5. "Thomas Accuser Defends Her Charge, and Herself," *New York Times*, October 8, 1991, A11.

6. In *Ellison v. Brady*, a 1991 U.S. Court of Appeals case, Judge Beezer wrote, "We adopt the perspective of a reasonable woman primarily because we believe that a sex-blind reasonable person standard tends to be male-biased and tends to systematically ignore the experiences of women. . . . [A] gender-conscious examination of sexual harassment enables women to participate in the workplace on an equal footing with men."

7. "Bush Emphasizes Support for Thomas in a High-Profile Meeting at White House," *New York Times*, October 10, 1991, A10.

8. Homi K. Bhabha, "A Good Judge of Character: Men, Metaphors, and the Common Culture," in Morrison, *Race-ing Justice*, 235, 247.

9. Rosemary L. Bray, "Taking Sides Against Ourselves," in Chrisman and Allen, *Court of Appeal*, 49.

10. Ibid., 53.

11. Nellie Y. McKay, "Remembering Anita Hill and Clarence Thomas: What Really Happened When One Black Woman Spoke Out," in Morrison, *Race-ing Justice*, 277.

12. Morrison, *Race-ing Justice*, xxix.

13. Nell Irvin Painter, "Hill, Thomas, and the Use of Racial Stereotype," in Morrison, *Race-ing Justice*, 200.

14. Christine Stansell, "White Feminists and Black Realities: The Politics of Authenticity," in Morrison, *Race-ing Justice*, 251.

15. This is the title of a book by bell hooks.

16. Stansell, "White Feminists," 254.

17. Ibid., 265.

(S)Mothering/Profess(or)ing

The two identities/jobs that most form my self-identity and most fill my time are those of mother and professor. In this essay I let my experiences in one inform those in the other. The main conversation here is a dialectic between public and private spheres, a dialectic that challenges that division even in the form of the essay: a personal piece on the politics of both realms.

Other conversations exist within the framework of that between spheres. I relate actual conversations I have had with my children and with my students (hopefully without embarrassing either). The public/private conversation mirrors and is mirrored in that between professor and mother. But what really gave rise to this essay was talking to myself, or myselves. I would like this to be read as a conversation between the multiple identities of a single self moving in a divided world. That's how I felt trying to sort out these ideas.

> If we are unable to resist and end domination in relations where there is care, it seems totally unimaginable that we can resist and end it in other institutionalized relations of power.
>
> bell hooks, *talking back*

11

🌿 🌿 🌿

(S)mothering/Profess(or)ing: Talking to Myself

Scene 1: My Life

"Mom, he hit me!"

"Penny, I feel like you're the only professor I can ask for help. My boyfriend hits me."

"I don't want to clean up, mom. You clean up."

"I don't want to get so involved in all this feminist stuff, Penny. But it's great that you enjoy the work."

"That's not fair, mom. I want to watch TV *now*."

"This grade isn't fair, Penny. I deserve better."

"Mom, I want to go out and play. Can I do my chores later?"

"Penny, I won't have my paper ready on time. Can I turn it in late?"

"Mom, how did the first people start?"

"Penny, how did sexism first start?"

"Mom, don't you know *anything*?"

"Penny, that is all just your opinion."

My students and my children come to me with conflicts, questions, demands for fairness and pleas for accommodation. Yet I was taught to believe that teaching students, especially college students, and being a parent, especially of young children, were pretty dissimilar tasks. Teaching was to take place in the public sphere, was paid labor, required a Ph.D. on my part, entailed promotions and

225

benefits, dubbed me a professional, and made my task the professional training of others. Mothering, on the other hand, belonged to the private sphere, was unpaid labor (in fact actually costs money!), required only the ordinary socialization to which most girls are subjected, entailed no promotions or benefits as those terms are usually understood, dubbed me not professional but "just a mother," and made my task one of nurturing little people into bigger ones. I find these familiar job descriptions so inaccurate, so unreflective of my practices, as to make me wonder on occasion whether I am "really" doing either one as they are "supposed" to be done. I want an understanding of my work that better matches my experiences, that allows for and makes sense of challenges to the traditional descriptions and practices, and that recognizes what I do as "really" doing it.

Being a mother and being a professor are the two most consuming occupations in my life. (I have stayed up half the night with sleepless children and with ungraded papers. I have mulled over and second guessed both how I answered a question in class and how I responded to the latest request for toys.) They are two endeavors with the most amazing ups and downs. ("Mommy, I love you." "Mommy, I hate you." "This class was the most meaningful one I have had in four years of college." "Professor Weiss grades too hard and is biased.") Each forms a large part of my self-identity and my public image. My practices in both are utterly informed by my feminism. I practice both in institutions not particularly to my liking.

The analogies are so easy to find it surprises me. Maybe anything could be made to fit into these sorts of comparisons. Perhaps because I am the same person mothering and professoring I turn both endeavors into the same kind of project. But maybe I am allowing myself to experiment with "hybrid" models: a professor who nurtures, a mother who asks for fairness; a professor who is connected, a mother who has political expectations. It is this experimental practice that I explore here, looking at specific incidents of interaction between the two.

Feminist analysis is crucial to understanding the tensions. Understanding the concrete struggles of those individuals working for change in restricted environments is crucial to developing that feminist analysis—is its point of departure. Here I use feminism to try to see not only how inequality in one arena (the academy) reinforces inequality in another (the family), but also how struggles for equality in each one have liberatory lessons for the other, and help to clarify questions as well as lead to some resolution. So I begin here with some of my own not very unique questions, frustrations, successes, and failures as a mother, and explore them by putting them in dialogue with my experiences as a teacher. And vice-versa.

Scene 2: Lost or Misplaced

I so often wonder what I am doing in academia and what I am doing in a family. As an academic I usually feel as if I don't fit in, and I worry about how much I should want to. I get disapproving glances for dressing so "casually," for cracking jokes at department meetings, for questioning what difference it makes to submit an article to this journal rather than that. I wonder what I am doing at conferences full of boys in corduroy jackets impressing each other with papers that lull me to sleep more often than they stir my imagination.

I sometimes feel lost in a family, as well. "Family," with a capital F. Something out there, not mine, to adapt to rather than to adapt to myself. (Like "University" with a capital U.) Something that forms my own and other people's perceptions and expectations of myself. As a mother I get disapproving glances for giving my children "too much" freedom, for taking motherhood/childhood so seriously, and for arguing for democratic families rather than father knows best. I wonder how to talk to other mothers as they live out and defend patriarchal family practices. And even though I am not married to my present partner, we are still this nice hetero couple with kids and cats and debts and dishes. A van and a man. I look so . . . so bourgeois, so straight, so middle-class.

I am the daughter of working class parents only one of whom finished high school. I am the daughter of parents who stayed together "for the kids." Perhaps these experiences helped form the basis for questioning the validity and self-importance of marriage and of higher education. Yet I cannot pretend that I am "in" these institutions and wholly not "of" them, as well, immune to internalization and accommodation. Too, I can not be in these institutions and not resist the person they assume and demand that I be. There is the common tension that both places and misplaces me.

Scene 3: Confrontation

Every day as class settles in, two students engage in rather loud laughter over who-knows-what. I try to keep my insecurity in check, stopping questions like: "Are they laughing about the class?" "Do they not take me or the course seriously"? I find myself getting more and more peeved about this as the weeks go on. About halfway through the semester I have my students meet with me individually. I tell one of the laughers that she comes across as not-very-serious the way she—dare I use the word?—giggles so in class. She is obviously taken aback. I am obviously nervous. I tell her I assume that she *is* serious, but that she is presenting herself in a way that undermines that.

It is not a comfortable conversation. I think I have offended her. But I have read a number of things she has written. She is very bright, expresses herself beautifully, has wonderful insights. I wonder if she has hidden her abilities and strengths behind her laughter, tried to make herself less believable and therefore more acceptable. It is a crummy bargain.

I have never engaged in this kind of direct behavioral challenge. I feel good that maybe she will think about conveying her strengths rather than sending mixed messages, probably messages that reflect mixed feelings and experiences. I think maybe no one has ever told her it is okay to be and to present herself as being competent.

And then I wonder who I think I am. What am I, her mother? Don't mothers worry about how their daughters will be perceived? Isn't it mothers who try to make daughters feel good about themselves? But do mothers confront their daughters this way? Do mothers make their daughters as uncomfortable as I have made this woman, as self-conscious? And, unlike her mother, I barely know her and will likely lose touch with her as she graduates from college.

Maybe this is an okay act of mothering/professoring without smothering. I treated her in some ways as a student: as a bright, aspiring, worthy learner. I was a teacher, trying to remove an obstacle to her aspirations. I was a mother: I *wanted* to help her get to where she wanted to be and had some suggestions, too. I was honest. Still, this seems more a personal than intellectual matter, as I was trained to worship the distinction. Removing something of the distance between us also felt draining. But so did avoiding the matter.

Scene 4: Power

There are times when mothering and professoring seem the same because they feel like two of the most undefinable, potentially endlessly expandable jobs in the world. Where all that I see when I look at the job description of each is DEMANDS. The students/children whine. They want more attention. They want less work. I'm not fair. I don't understand. The stuff I ask them to do is too hard. They want to play something else.

I teach at a large university, where many of the students are attention starved. The undergraduates want a professor to talk to them about future jobs, graduate school possibilities, how they can get an 'A,' what they should do about their boyfriend's sexism, a paper for another class, the time they were raped, something from my class they loved or hated or got confused or turned on by. The graduate students want to talk about how difficult a time they are having in graduate school, a conference they went to, a paper they are thinking about trying to get published, how to be a professor and a parent and politically active, graduate exams, an incompetent or sexist professor, job possibilities for a lesbian interested in lesbian studies, a book I haven't read.

I have three children. While they are not attention starved, there seems to me to be no natural limit to the amount of attention they are interested in having, at least as relative youngsters. I'm hungry. I want to read to you. I want you to read to me. My owie hurts. I want to plan a birthday party. Help me with my homework. Draw with me. Let's make up a story. Push me on the swing. Help me find my shoes. I want to play with play-dough *now*. Teach me how to play the recorder. Hold me. Let's make cookies. Want to play a game with me? Let's go for a bike ride.

The similarity here makes no sense. How often have I read (or said) that teacher is to student as parent is to child as male is to female and relatively powerful is to relatively powerless? Though on the top half of at least two of these fractions, I don't feel powerful. I feel frazzled, more often than not. And if my child is upset at me I don't blow it off as if I were an unaccountable powerholder ruling these inferior children in my own interest. If a student thinks I was unfair I don't assume she's wrong, as if I were an infallible and irresponsible giver of my wisdom teaching what I care about the way I want to teach it. While mothers are talked about as potentially smothering creatures, as a mother/professor I feel better described as always potentially and usually in fact smothered. Based on the extent to which my children and students speak, in agreement with, in conversation with, and in challenge of me, the analogy of teacher/student with rulers/subjects does not capture the entirety of their experience either. Still, I think I am more distant from my supposed role than they are from theirs. Why is that, and what are the implications?

A student tells me in my office that I have silenced her. I did so by disagreeing with her in class. Is that the power I have? Where did I get it? Sitting in a classroom in graduate school? Going through graduation for the Ph.D.? Getting handed the gradebook upon arrival at the university? And where did she lose herself to the extent that a disagreement with me over an article leaves her silenced, put down, furious at me yet barely able to express it months later? I hate this set-up. *I* don't want to play anymore. Everything feels like such an enormous amount of work, and the seemingly smallest misstep can have such damaging consequences. I think about the power I have over my children, too. I can give and take away, make decisions about their clothes, their toys, their schools. Where did I get such power? When I was pregnant? The moment they separated from my body? Over the years of caring for them? Perhaps more importantly, how do I get rid of it? How can they not know that I am just forging through the day's decisions imperfectly even if conscientiously?

Scene 5: Pain

She writes to me in her journal about the story we read of a woman who lost her voice because of a violent sexual assault. Only the woman in bell hooks' story says it's because something happened to her, you know, they made her do things. She can't use the word rape in the story. And my student can't use the word rape in her journal. She just says it happened to her, too. And she *still* can't speak about it.

I sit with her journal in front of me wondering what to write. I sit thinking that there seems to be no end to the stories of violations my students share with me. Every semester I hear of rapes and sexual harassment, of incest and battery. There are other stories, too, not of violation in the same sense but of traumas. Of the inability of a lesbian student to come out to friends or family. Of the breakup of a relationship because her discovery of feminism was something he didn't bargain for. Of an abortion. Of an eating disorder.

There are students who have trusted me with information they say they have trusted very few others with—sometimes, in fact, not anyone. They need to hear certain things in response to that telling, things that will help them, that will bolster their strength. Will I find the words? They need very much just to be heard and believed. I think how there is no one who is unscarred.

I try to make sure they know about support groups, self-defense classes, practicing saying no, expressing what it is they *do* want, useful books that at least provide a framework for understanding what happened. But they will never "get over" what has happened to them, and they cannot be guaranteed future safety. I certainly cannot give them that.

I think about my kids, and the hurts they will suffer, that I as a feminist know they will suffer. The hurts that I cannot protect them from no matter what I do, because I cannot keep them immune from that which is pervasive. This makes a farce of the whole notion of protecting one's children, at least in a patriarchy. It is a farce because their sacrifice and pain will be required. Will someone be sitting with my child's journal fifteen years from now reading of their pain? And, if so, will that professor be enough of a mother to treat it tenderly, to cherish the child?

Scene 6: A Good Fit

I had an opportunity that was so wonderful, that came about and went well *because* I am a mother professor. I got to do the first of a series of special classes at the new alternative school in town, a class for 8- to 12-year-olds on gender and race issues. My three kids are in the school, a school I helped found. One teacher, knowing of my affiliation with Women's Studies at work and with all things equity-related at the school, came to me with a gender-based conflict that had emerged in her room. (It seems that while building equipment on the playground the boys claimed exclusive ownership of certain jobs and tools.) Well, the discussion I had with the kids kept me high all day. I was amazed by how frank they were, sharing stories in front of their friends of times when they had been made fun of for doing something that crossed gender boundaries. I was reaffirmed by the evidence they gave that even from the very youngest of ages children are aware of and hurt by the injustices of gender roles and inequality. Given more evidence that children are in fact wrestling with what they see around them, I was convinced of the urgency of teaching an anti-bias curriculum to youngsters. I was impressed with the speed and depth of their understanding of the injustices. Today I am hopeful—it does happen—and happy to be a professoring mother.

Scene 7: Difference

Today I was reading the kids the story "Else-Marie and the Seven Little Daddies." It's a weird story, really, about a child who is worried about her little fathers picking her up from school for the first time when all the other kids have just one big daddy. The kids and I were in the bed reading, and for us it was a relatively calm time. When the story was over I said something about how the story was about worrying about being different. I told how sometimes I worried about being different, and gave as an example being vegetarian (figuring they could expand it). I said people often asked me why I didn't eat meat, and sometimes I worried what they were thinking. I also said that over the years many of my friends have become vegetarian, and that my being a veg was one influence on them, which made me feel good. So here I was, hoping for a chance to talk about being different, and the two older ones take off out of the room like someone just pushed the EJECT button. Avi, on the the other hand, newly turned 3, had lots of questions.

I think about their little minds grappling with what they know are not easy issues. They have no doubt already realized that most of the people they know eat meat, abide by sex roles, and play with guns and Barbies, just to mention some of the more obvious gaps. They know they are different. But they also know they are not alone: they have friends in their alternative school who are vegetarian, and they join other children at the annual Take Back the Night marches, for example. I wish it were easier to figure out how to talk to them about this stuff. In my best understanding of what happened I think, "Well, they heard what I said, and at some level that's what's important. They have those words in their head to wrestle with when they want or need to. And only they can judge the right times. They are not obliged to join a conversation about it because I am ready for it." In my more paranoid moments I think, "Oh, they're already tired of this, and they're so young. I don't know anything about how to present this in a way they can hear it and use it, or a way that opens things up for them to say, 'Yeah, one day so-and-so said she thought it was weird that I didn't eat meat.'"

I wonder what it is like to be a five-year-old girl who wants Barbies and dresses like the other girls and to have a mother who says dresses aren't great play clothes, and who refuses to spend money on dolls with hair down to their butts standing on their tip-toes? I wonder what it is like to be a seven-year-old boy who watches the other boys play only with boys and wear super-hero clothes and sport super-soaker guns, and to have a mother who insists that girls and boys be invited over to play, who bans the appearance of vio- lent figures on underwear or t-shirts, and who sends out party invi- tations with the caveat: "Please: no war toys!"?

Letting this mother-wonder inform my professor-wonder, I am struck that my students have similar dilemmas. What is it like to go to a frat party and realize that the boys you went there to party with are making harassing comments like those you studied in feminist theory class last week? What do you do? Go along, or say nothing, or pretend that he really doesn't mean anything bad, or suppress your own discomfort? Or do you assert yourself, your new-found and still shaky feminist identity, and thereby make your difference visible and undoubtedly the subject of not-so-friendly comments? What is it like to live in that frat house and see the pornography going around, and know from your "Women and the Law" class about the nature and effects of pornography? Will you ask for a house meeting about it, or an educational program on the subject? Will you be that visibly in resistance, or will you just pass the stuff on, or maybe silently throw it away when it comes to you?

I have to know in all these cases that resistance is difficult, and its costs are often more visible than the costs of going along, its benefits often less immediate. Each of us has to be allowed time to grow into our own approaches to dealing with the grief we get for our politics. After twenty years as a political activist, certain acts are habits to me that are new territory for many of my students and my children. When I treat working with them as new territory for me, when I continue to confront new challenges, I am reminded of how tenderness and vulnerability mix with commitment and strength, and of how important being respected in the process feels.

Scene 8: Smothered

One semester I began by inviting a discussion of male bashing. I thought that we could clear up from the start how what we do in class differs from what they call male bashing. (Hope springs eter- nal.) Their definitions focused on such things as "generalizing

about all males," and "blaming men for everything." I ask for concrete examples. I call on a woman with her hand raised. She says,
"I know people won't agree with me, but . . ." I'm flabbergasted. I
interrupt: "It's the first day of class! How do you know what anyone
in here thinks?" "Well," she replies, "I've been in classes like this
before." The next week the issue of housework somehow comes up.
A student says, "You know, sometimes it's women's fault. They
don't let men help in the home, don't want them to." "Why do you
think that is?" I ask her. "Well, the way we treat things in here,
you'll say it's because she was socialized." This time I don't ask her
how she knows, in the second week of class, "how we treat things
in here" or what I'll say. It's not relevant. Her image of a feminist
is running the class. I am a mouthpiece, a straw person.

There's so much self-righteousness in the opposition—they're so
certain they have found the flaws in feminist thinking. "Okay!" they
want to hear. "It's true! Feminists have thoughtlessly taken positions on issues that only exist because we make mountains out of
molehills. We destroy women by blaming men for everything. Our
party line of political correctness cleverly keeps both feminists and
antifeminists in line. And yes, we want women to be treated better
than men." Is there such a thing as feminist bashing?

One of the practices people often question me about concerns
guns. The rule in our house is simple: no guns, no gun games allowed. Pretending guns are toys makes them seem innocent. We
normalize killing by making games of it. "Oh, it's normal for children to play gun games," I hear more often than I ever imagined.
"You can't mold your kids," I am warned in serious tones. "Don't
force your values on them." The certainty with which this advice is
offered, and the active hostility to my positions (real and imagined),
is stark.

I get tired. Every time I sit down to eat with someone for the first
time I get asked not only "Why are you a vegetarian," but get
quizzed on everything from whether I think plants have feelings to
what I would do if stranded on an island where the only chance of
survival was to kill and eat a cow. I am considered rude or gross if
I ask them why they eat meat, whether they know about factory
farms, or why they find it acceptable to eat cows and pigs but not

horses or cats? I have to explain my children's haircuts, names, dress, toys, lack of TV, etc., and *the* feminist position on everything from abortion to affirmative action.

To smother: "to overcome or kill with smoke or fumes; to destroy the life of by depriving of air; to overcome or discomfit through or as if through lack of air; . . . to suppress expression or knowledge of; . . . to cover thickly." Mothers have been warned not to smother their children—one of the many missteps we might take. Professors are not usually warned not to smother their students. Perhaps we should be, since many teachers, especially of graduate students, try very hard to create students in their own images, and put so many demands on them as to leave little time for life outside the laboratory or library.

Why is anyone smothered? For the self-interest of the smotherer, or to validate smotherers by having others conform. To limit, cover-up, or destroy. That is what oppression does, but the meaning is more political: "to crush or burden by abuse of power or authority; to burden spiritually or mentally: weigh heavily upon." The smothering of patriarchal institutions is covered up, and therefore generally invisible. The attempt to resist such smothering, such confinement and destruction, is called: oppressing white men, forcing children to conform, caring too much, going too far. Go figure.

Final Thoughts

To teach and to rear children, to rear students and to teach children, are sometimes spoken of as opportunities to mold young minds. As a feminist mother professor I also see them as opportunities to remove the mold from their minds, to help them break the mold. While teaching college and helping children grow often seem so ill-defined, so endlessly demanding, so boundary-less, I know that in most ways the issue is not these particular jobs. Feminist movement shakes things up. Feminists engage in struggle. It happened when I waited tables, worked in a day care center, and worked at a women's shelter.

I know we have the power to question, resist, and recreate. I hear the questions every day, from my children and students. I witness them taking risks against discrimination. I know I am privileged to see and hear their stories as they learn, dare, fail, rage, cry, try again, laugh, and prevail. The nature of these relationships and processes means that as a mother/professor I both comfort and discomfort, nurture and confront, challenge and support. I am often wrong and often wise. Usually I care, but sometimes I turn it off. Sometimes I love my jobs, and sometimes I hate them, occasionally at the same time. Among my resources, I can look from mothering to professoring, and the reverse, for consolation, recognition, or solution.

Note

Reprinted with permission from *Feminist Teacher* 9, 3 (Spring/Summer 1995): 137–42.

Index

About the Author

Penny Weiss is associate professor of political science at Purdue University in West Lafayette, Indiana. She is author of *Gendered Community: Rousseau, Sex, and Politics,* and co-editor, with Marilyn Friedman, of *Feminism and Community.* Her academic research now is on the history of feminist theory. Most of her time outside of academia is spent either weeding her vegetable garden or volunteering at the alternative school her children attend.